Enjoy!

Warren Berland

"Dr. Berland has developed a simple step by step program that will move you rapidly to a state of freedom and choice, bringing you a sense of tremendous well being."

—Robert Shaw, M.D., Medical Director, the Family Institute of Berkeley

"Warren Berland has written a deceptively simple, wonderfully practical book for folks interested in generative living. I highly recommend this book to you, as I will recommend it to clients of mine."

—Stephen Gilligan, Ph.D., Psychotherapist, author, *The Courage to Love*

"A liberating, clear-eyed, and open-hearted approach to peace of mind, body, and spirit. *Out of the Box for Life* is especially useful to those many people who still feel stuck after years of therapy."

—Henry Dreher, author of *The Immune Power Personality*

"Among all the books on self-care and health, *Out of the Box for Life* is a stand-out. Berland's deep grounding and thorough research are evident on every page, and the sensitive, practical program is sure to make a difference in many lives."

—Dr. Dennis T. Jaffe, author of *Healing from Within*

"*Out of the Box for Life* is both practical and profound, and I am certainly pleased to recommend it."

—O. Carl Simonton, M.D. author of *Getting Well Again*

Contents

Acknowledgments

The idea of a book was conceived one afternoon on Cape Cod with Bill and Steffanie O'Hanlon. I will always be grateful to them for their help and encouragement.

Many colleagues, family and friends played an invaluable role in helping to write this book. They offered numerous meaningful and insightful suggestions. Among those I want to especially acknowledge are: Barbara Altman Bruno, Ilene Berland-Calabrese, Fred Calabrese, Bob Carroll, Henry Dreher, Lisa Halprin, Roberta Halsey, Ed Klein, Phyllis Kornfeld, Elizabeth O'Conner, Janet Paul, Chana and Hank Strauss, and Roz Wolff.

My agent, Loretta Barrett, immediately recognized the value of this work both for herself and others, and found the right home for it.

My editor, Megan Newman, offered inspiring suggestions that greatly enhanced the quality and clarity of this book. Her enthusiasm for the work made our collaboration a truly wonderful experience.

My teachers, Andrew Cohen, Dr. Larry LeShan, Dr. Bob Shaw and Dr. Bernie Siegel, taught me the extraordinary, limitless possibility that dwells within each of us to live deeply meaningful lives. I sincerely hope that through this book, many people will become aware of the profound spiritual understandings of Andrew Cohen.

My mother, Sylvia, and my late father, Jack, taught me compassion and that one's life should make a difference in the lives of others.

Acknowledgments

I humbly thank the many clients with whom I have worked over the past two decades for trusting me with their most personal concerns. It is from their lives that the examples in this book were drawn. (To protect their anonymity, their names and other identifying information have been changed.) They taught me how best to work with them to resolve their issues and discover who they really are. With them I formulated and fine-tuned the processes in this book. I thank them for their openness, compassion, and willingness to make profound changes in their lives. From their strength many others may too find fulfillment in their lives.

Finally, it is with deep gratitude and love that I thank my wife, Joan, for the immeasurable ways she supported me during the writing of this book—with her love, encouragement, time, and extraordinarily good food. Beyond that, she consistently and tirelessly found ways to clarify and simplify my writing, and regularly amazed both of us with the brilliant words and ideas that came out of her mouth. I will always treasure our joyful partnership.

Part I

Introduction

There is a place in all of us that has remained innocent, uncorrupted and untouched by the world. We have to locate that most delicate place. It is a very sensitive place, it's where we feel love—where tenderness and compassion arise, free from self-interest.

—ANDREW COHEN, *ENLIGHTENMENT IS A SECRET*

What if the key to living a healthy, happy, satisfying life were already in your possession and always had been? What if this kind of life could be easily accessed? What if you were free of your insecurities, doubts, and fears? What if the only thing you needed were the right tools?

I'm writing this book to tell you exactly what those tools are and precisely how to use them. You may have searched everywhere—in money, success, relationships—and come away feeling disappointed and empty. You haven't failed. You've simply been unaware that the key to finding the satisfaction you desire is right inside you, where it's always been.

In many ways, we are all like Dorothy in *The Wizard of Oz,* searching all over to find our way home. Although she didn't realize it, all Dorothy had to do was click her heels three times to get there. She always had that power. She just didn't know it.

Like Dorothy, you probably never dreamed that getting home to your true self could be so simple.

I won't be asking you to click your heels. But I will be asking you to shift the way you look at things. It may be a little more difficult than heel-clicking, but believe me, the results can be as immediate and startling as Dorothy's swift return home.

This shift in perspective may be thought of in spiritual, psychological, or in very practical terms. Either way, it reveals a simple truth: All we need to solve our problems with wisdom and understanding is to return to our true self. And this can be accomplished once we make the choice to be who we really are rather than who our self-image says we are.

When you come home to yourself, to your own *true* self, you can live your life free of emotional pain, fear, anger, and despair. When people ask, "How are you?" your natural response will be "Better than I ever thought possible." And you'll really mean it. You will have chosen to tap into that place where living a wonderful life is the real truth, and pain and suffering is the lie.

This book is about finding the place within yourself that expresses your true nature and learning how to connect with it at any time under any circumstances.

From this place, an entirely new view of the world will emerge that is unencumbered by doubt, fear, and insecurity. This is the place where you can escape from self-imposed limitations and be free, perhaps for the first time.

You need no previous psychotherapy, no years of spiritual training. You don't need the right childhood, the right parents, money, or fame. You don't have to become more loving, less angry, or less self-centered in order to use this process. But once you learn how to use the tools in this book, you will change in many wonderful ways.

A New Psychotherapy

By training, I am a psychotherapist. I spent the first four years of my practice using a traditional approach to therapy based on the assumption that our true nature is determined by what has happened in our past. The assumption was that if we understood the psychological reasons for our fears, worries, anxieties, and anger, we could solve those problems. I was taught that the solution to problems could be found by answering two questions: "What is wrong with you?" and "How did you get that way?"

These two questions become the focus of many who go into therapy. Some people spend much of their lives trying to figure out the source of their problems. Nonetheless, this approach has yielded precious little in genuine understanding about how we change and get better. I believe that this is because its foundation is significantly flawed. The problem is the presumption that our self-image, otherwise known as the ego, represents our true nature. And it truly doesn't.

In reality, the ego is a veil that obscures who we really are. Our true nature resides just below the ego and is completely immune to whatever has scarred it. Therefore our attempts to heal ourselves by treating the ego miss the point and leave us mired in the same mess. The fact is, the path to our true selves is around the swampy dark forest of the ego, not through it.

Fortunately, in 1980 I met and trained with a brilliant therapist named Dr. Bob Shaw. What I learned at his seminar entitled "Mastery in Psychotherapy" forever changed the way I worked with clients and lived my life.

I discovered that not only were we *choosing* to view life from the perspective of limiting, confining, and imprisoning beliefs but that we could make a different choice and see that same life from a perspective that sets us free. It is a perspective that reveals the magnificence and fullness of everything around us. It is the source of emotional well-being and creativity as well as the reflection of our true nature.

After working with Dr. Shaw, I returned to my practice in New York and, applying what I had learned, completed work with 90 percent of my clients within three weeks. In that time, I taught them how to examine what was healthy and positive about themselves rather than focusing on what was wrong. In less than a month they didn't need me, or any other psychotherapist, because they were no longer operating from the misconception that they were damaged and needed to be fixed. They realized that what they were searching for, a sense of freedom and contentment, was waiting there within them. Each and every one of us can do the same.

Got a Problem? Need a Solution?

Fortunately for everyone, the field of psychotherapy has progressed over the past ten years to encompass a more solution-oriented approach. A number of therapists, such as Bill O'Hanlon, who has written fifteen books including *Love Is a Verb* and *In Search of Solutions* (co-written with Michele Weiner-Davis), have led the way. Here is the foundation of this approach:

- Understanding the "origins" of a problem is of little practical use in resolving it. Although we can come to some understanding of how a problem may have begun, that does little to help us begin to act differently.

- Change does not have to take time.

- Solving one problem does not create another.

- "Resistance" to change during psychotherapy is often due to the way the therapist approaches the "problem" rather than to a deficit within the client. When given the proper tools, people want to change, they do change, and the changes can be permanent.

Finding a New Path

On my own journey of self-discovery, I began to search for a way to access and remain my true self. One of the first and most useful books for me at that time was Steven Levine's *A Gradual Awakening*. Often I would choose a passage from his book that I wanted to deeply understand. Then I would simply sit and write, sometimes up to ten pages, as a way to expand my understanding and embody what he had discussed. I would not stop until I felt I fully knew what he meant by a particular statement or passage. It was satisfying to reach these most profound levels of awareness. I still recommend that people use writing as a contemplative activity and that they don't stop until they experience a shift in their awareness.

As time went on, I became more able to trust and enter into a state where I could see things as they truly were, undistorted by the ego. I began to understand that this place was always there, and that it was possible to access it with only the intention to do so. Because it is separate from the distortions of the ego, it produces a profound clarity. I term this place where clarity resides the *true self*.

I began to expect and demand that I be in that state before beginning any client session. I believed that nothing less was appropriate for the responsibility I felt. I often walked around my apartment in New York City asking myself questions such as "What if I were clear right now? What would I see? How would I feel? What would I be experiencing?" It often did the trick to shift my perspective into a place where I felt free and open to all possibilities. My stance became what Dr. Bob Shaw called being "light-footed."

I felt that if I were unwavering in my commitment to remain free and clear, then I could lead my clients to their own clarity and the resolution of their problems. It was a wonderful way to work because it was so filled with possibility. I knew that if I could generate this perspective, then anyone could.

Soon I began to wonder why people should have to continue to visit me in order to find themselves. I also felt that having this wonderful experience should not be limited to once a week. It was, after all, always available. I was committed to finding a way for people to access it on their own. Then Robert came to see me and I saw the way.

My session with Robert is one I will never forget. Robert was a thirty-eight-year-old married man who was suffering from a general sense of malaise. He felt stuck, frustrated, and powerless. Talking about it didn't seem to further our understanding of the situation or give him relief.

In an attempt to shed light on the true source of his difficulty, I first asked him a simple question: "What if you were stuck in a box and couldn't get out? How would you be experiencing life?" He said that he would feel trapped and hopeless, much the way he felt right now. I agreed that it did seem to describe how he was viewing life. The box seemed to be the perfect metaphor for how Robert (and most of us) lived life.

I then wanted him to begin to envision a way out, to a place that was free of his sense of limitation and hopelessness. So I said, "Imagine that you are out of the box and experiencing a sense of total freedom. How would life look then?"

From that perspective of freedom and possibility, he was immediately able to examine various issues in a way that was undistorted by his suffering. He was thrilled by the ease with which he could look at everything from a totally new perspective, one that was unavailable just a moment before. For the first time he experienced freedom from his haunting, demoralizing thoughts. He saw that many of his issues were the result of looking at life from a sense of being "in the box" and that once he was "out of the box," he could choose a very different way of responding. His only responsibility was to honor what he had recognized from this perspective.

The methods and philosophy that form the essence of this book are a synthesis of my work over the past decade and a half. During that period, I realized that at times of confusion, pain, and crisis, people tend to seek a deeper understanding of and connection with themselves, with others, with God, and with the meaning of life.

This was especially evident in my doctoral research with those who unexpectedly survived cancer. For them, a new appreciation and understanding of life was seen as an important part of their healing. Despite the extraordinary challenge that the illness presented, many people also described how the quality of their lives remarkably improved.

Doris, a fifty-four-year-old woman who was given a year to live twenty-three years ago and who has since became a spiritual psychotherapist, said:

> There's a power within you; it is untapped in most of us, and yes, you do have power. Yes, you do have control. Not just of your medical treatment and choices. It is a kind of recentering. Connecting with yourself is the only way. I feel the responsibility to have others explore where their connection is. It can be playing golf or going to church, I don't know. Whatever gives you that, you have to find it. Then you have to take it with you wherever you go during the day. It has to become part of you.

It is a question of understanding that we are never free from our bondage to our human experience. It is understanding that the work never stops, because I hear that so many times—people say, "How long will it take?" You see, it will take a lifetime. And every step is a step. There is no beginning and no end.

This example reaffirms much of what this book is about— that each of us can choose to live a meaningful, satisfying life that expresses the best of what human beings are made of.

If you are looking for a method to move you forward with personal, relationship, work, or health issues, you have come to the right place. If you are looking for spiritual guidance, you will find it on almost every page that you read. If you are a business executive, educator, or therapist, you will learn a powerfully effective approach for helping others access their own source of creativity, integrity, strength, and independence. Whatever your purpose, wherever you are in your life, this process can help you, and those with whom you relate, find the way to a fulfilling life.

It is amazingly easy, quite practical, and fun. It will help you resolve the most difficult problems, communicate more effectively in your relationships, deepen your creativity, live a healthier life, find the true source of love, and discover finally who you are—and can be. It is designed to give you practical information, exercises, and inspiring examples of others who have used the out-of-the-box process to resolve the most challenging issues of life. I invite you to approach the ideas and exercises in this book as an explorer—be passionate and open to whatever you discover about yourself— about life.

In time you will come to understand that you can access a

deeper source of wisdom, satisfaction, and joy than you thought possible when you were being controlled by your limited, fearful ego. No therapist is necessary. No training is necessary. When you experience being free from the ego, you will know what is possible. All the answers you need will be at your fingertips, if you are willing to look from this perspective. You will need nothing else.

Being free is always a choice, no matter how stuck you feel or how distant the possibility appears. It is always close at hand, waiting for you. When you surrender to that fact alone, you are making room inside for this deepest knowing to come through.

What you discover is a sense of freedom and possibility that can be found in each moment. You alone must take the first step to be free. Each time you do, you reinforce and strengthen your resolve, and your confidence grows. Surrender to this inner knowing, and you become the instrument of good. You have found your true self, and from here you get the answers you need. Freedom is your choice—any time, any place, and under any circumstances.

Achieve this and you also achieve something else: you help raise the standard for all humankind. In setting yourself free, if only for a moment, you take everyone a step forward. As when the four-minute mile was first run, a new possibility arises for everyone. Your triumph becomes our triumph. The implications are extraordinarily profound.

In generations to come, I believe that this will be recognized as the turning point in our quest for wholeness. You will have been at the forefront of the next great leap in our human development. There is no greater calling, and no greater reward. From out of the box, it is obvious that this is so. You will know that you are a part of something much larger than yourself, and you will naturally care more for the whole. The potential for deeper human connection can then become a reality. I welcome you on this journey back to yourself, and deeply respect the fact that you care enough to set out on this voyage. The possibilities are endless.

1

The True Self

The Place Untouched by Trauma, Fear, and History

> The instant we stop serving the self-image [the ego] and its needs, all our difficulties disappear, and our energy is released to flow smoothly. This energy can then be used to further enhance our understanding of ourselves. . . .
>
> Remember it is your self-image that is unhappy, not you.
>
> —TARTHANG TULKU, *OPENNESS MIND*

Ego 101

As we set out on this journey, I want to clarify one thing—we all have an ego. According to Webster's Dictionary, ego is "the part of the psyche [mind] that experiences and reacts to the outside world." According to Freudian thought, it develops early in life, and its primary function is to protect us from a sense of vulnerability and emotional pain. That sense of vulnerability is what causes us to look outside ourselves for stability, acknowledgment, love, and happiness.

To protect ourselves from feeling or revealing our vulnerability, we develop many ways to keep ourselves insulated from criticism, judgment, abandonment, and hurt. The most common way is to seek safety in the arms of the ego because it feels as if it protects us from the unpleasantness of life.

I see the ego in a totally different light. By my definition, the ego is a constricted part of the personality that we think of as ourselves and where a sense of limitation dwells. It is a plastic mask that we wear to give us the illusion of protection but that really just limits what we can see, feel, and experience. It is also a veil that obscures our deeper and truer selves by keeping us caught up in needless suffering, terrible self-consciousness, doubt, guilt, fear, and worry. It demands our attention and keeps us focusing on what is wrong. In reality, the ego does not protect us—it controls us, unless we learn how to put it in its place.

In this book, you will learn to shift from the ego's perspective of negativity, insecurity, doubt, and misperceptions to one that reflects your true self, which is marked by wisdom, the ability to love, and an unshakable feeling of emotional well-being. The implications of following the techniques described can be profound. You will soon be able to live your life from the true source of your happiness and fulfillment. You'll know that the first step toward being free is to choose to be.

Our True Self, Untouched by Life

> I am convinced that there is another realm to experience when we are ready to go beyond this life to which we have become accustomed. This other realm defies our laws of science and logic. It is a place within each of us that is free of ordinary boundaries, rules, and limitations.
>
> —WAYNE DYER

The perspective I am discussing can be described as untouched by anything that has happened to us in the past.

Why this is true remains a mystery and can't yet be explained, but this place in us simply can't be and has never been affected by past trauma or emotional upsets in our lives. This place is completely immune to our limited, psychologically oriented view of ourselves and to any hurt the ego has received. So rather than trying to fix our personality by looking for answers to our emotional and physical well-being outside of ourselves, we can simply access that part of ourselves where freedom from limitations exists. From that vantage point, we will actually see a completely different world, and experience ourselves in a radically new light. That part of ourselves is also the place where the deepest expression of love and caring can be found. I call this place the true self.

Therefore I am proposing an entirely new approach to change. It is grounded in the belief that we can discover our true nature, and from that perspective we can solve any emotional issues in our life. Following are the ten fundamental tenets on which this understanding is based:

1. We are not our thoughts or our feelings.

2. The ego, intent on maintaining its rigid control, will do all it can to hide this understanding so that it can dominate our life.

3. When we step back from the ego, our mistaken assumptions about ourselves and life will be revealed.

4. Once they are revealed, the ego will be exposed as a misguided and self-centered illusion that demands and consumes all of our attention.

5. Shifting to the perspective of the true self is simple with the right tools and the intention to do so.

6. Our true self is already there waiting and yearning to be found.

7. The true self is accessible at all times and in all circumstances.

8. The true self is separate from anything that has ever happened to us and therefore unscarred by it.

9. When we are living from our true self, nothing is ever wrong, so nothing needs to be fixed.

10. Being our true self will reveal our love, our wisdom, our compassion, and our life purpose.

What You Are Looking for Is You

What if you already had the key to unlock aspects of yourself that you never knew existed? What if you have already done so in your life? What was revealed to you at those moments? Did you experience a subtle or profound shift in your sense of self?

It may have been a time when you felt you were free from your usual way of being or had experienced a deeper sense of connection with another person, to nature, to God, to music, to a piece of art, or to something else that had great meaning for you. Perhaps you sensed a feeling of oneness or experienced a loss of self-consciousness or a total involvement in what you were doing. You might have been "lost" in a sports activity such as skiing or tennis, been consumed by a creative activity like writing or painting, or experienced a moment of deep gratitude or love.

These moments, which regretfully last for all too short a period of time, reveal that there is another way of experiencing yourself and life. You may not have grasped the implications of these experiences, but you know that they were real. You know that you tasted something wonderful.

At these times you might recognize that you are more confident, secure, loving, content, free, at ease, and happy. What if this is really who you are? What if you were actually getting a glimpse into something quite extraordinary about yourself? What would that say about who you are? What would it say about how you can live your life? I suggest that you begin to consider this possibility by asking yourself these very questions.

This book will help you answer these questions and, if taken seriously, will provide a road map for your return home to your true self. I assure you that there is an unimaginable source of freedom, joy, and strength on the other side of your doubts and fears, just waiting to be expressed. All your true self needs is for you to set it free.

Maybe you've never experienced moments of freedom, or you feel that this perspective is unattainable at this moment. Possibly you're hearing your ego object, "No, this can't work for me because there is something very wrong with me. I am too insecure-weak-fat-short-hopeless-unlovable [fill in the blank]." It could also be saying, "It can't be this easy or everyone would already be doing it." You will learn ways to recognize and disregard these expressions of doubt and fear as the calling card of the ego. You will then begin to focus on what you want from life rather than on what's wrong, and you won't stop until you get it.

Feelings will no longer grip or control you, because you will make the choice about how to respond to them. This will be true even in the most difficult, seemingly impossible circumstances. What's more, doing so will be fun. I know that it sounds too good to be true, but it isn't.

We will discover that freedom is a choice, and happiness is a choice. Being who we are each and every day is a choice. It is simply a choice like turning on a light so that we can see or drinking water to relieve our thirst. It is a choice that we can make anytime, anywhere, under any circumstances. What is experienced at these wondrous moments of coming into contact with our true self is the realization that this perspective has always been there and can never be lost.

What we need for this journey is a sincere commitment to wanting to end our suffering, and the willingness to discover places we never knew existed. What it comes down to, and this is the splendor of the process, is making the choice to leave our pain behind so that we can finally have a life we might only have dreamed possible.

2

Being In the Box

> Reality is simply the loss of the ego. Destroy the ego by
> seeking its identity. It will automatically vanish and re-
> ality will shine forth by itself. This is the direct method.
> —Ramana Maharshi, *The Enlightened Mind*
> (Stephen Mitchell, ed.)

It's time for us to experience being "in the box." To help,
here is a useful tip from a client who long ago mastered this
process. He said about the process, "You are asked to describe how you are feeling and what you are thinking. When
you try to evade by intellectualizing, you are gently reminded, 'No, I want you to fully experience being in the box.'
You have no choice but to feel the feelings."

Please take his advice, and take the time to experience what
I am suggesting. It will help a great deal in developing your
ability to distinguish this new perspective from your usual way
of being and will also help you realize when the in-the-box
perspective is running you. Here is the first part of the process.

Being In the Box

*Imagine that you are stuck in a small box and cannot get
out. You're unable to see and unable to move. Feel the walls
closing in on you. How does it feel being trapped inside?
What are you thinking about? What are you feeling?*

Imagine that the wall in front of you is a wall of your nega-

tive beliefs about yourself and your life. The wall behind you is a wall of your fears, your insecurities, and your self-doubts. The wall to your right is your concerns about your future and your fears that things will get worse. The wall to the left is your negative feelings about your past. Imagine that the low ceiling above you is filled with your memories of what people have done to you. Imagine that the floor beneath you holds your anger and resentments. Get the picture?

Take a few minutes to fully experience the sense of being stuck or trapped in this box with all of these thoughts and feelings pressing in on you. Then feel your emotional reac-tion—your frustration, hopelessness, anger, powerlessness, fear, and feelings of being overwhelmed by it all. Imagine this until you feel these sensations inside your body.

The experience of being in the box is to a greater or lesser extent the way many people experience life. They feel power-less to overcome life's difficulties and unable to get beyond their feelings and reactions to these dilemmas. Instead their emotions are triggered by things that happen to them. For example, if your spouse yells at you for not taking out the garbage, it is difficult not to respond defensively, angrily, or by feeling hurt. Your reaction somehow seems to be more im-portant and powerful than your desire to resolve the situa-tion. You probably haven't even considered the possibility that there is a need for another response.

Similarly, if your boss criticizes your work, it is difficult to imagine that you could choose to feel any way other than hurt or angry, much less get completely free from any feeling whatsoever.

If you think you don't have enough money, you might think that is the reason you are upset or unhappy. Or if your friend does not return your phone call for several days, you might feel that your hurt or anger is justified. You may feel resigned or discouraged about it, you may feel that they have ruined your day, and you may feel that you have little choice but to react in whatever negative way you have. In each of these scenarios, it appears that your responses are determined by an event rather than by you.

Don't Believe Everything You Think

Many of us spend the majority of our lives stuck in a box. What is worse is that we do not even know we are in one.

Unfortunately, getting in the box is very easy to do. The ego, which can perceive only from a limited viewpoint, is the lens through which we see life. When the ego feels fear or is threatened, it instantly resorts to its tried-and-true methods to guard us from danger or potential pain.

Although this reaction serves a purpose in certain life-threatening situations, like a physical assault, most of the time the perceived threat is to our pride or self-image. So we live in fear of our shadow. We are afraid that something will pierce the armor that protects us from being seen as we believe we are, with all our perceived flaws. We don't want others to know that we are anxious or insecure or that there is something "wrong" with our body. We then berate ourselves for feeling this way in the first place.

The funniest part is that each of us is doing the same thing. We think that we are alone in this behavior, that we have a worse case of insecurity, doubt, or fear than anyone else. Although some of us are more focused on these concerns, we all do it to some degree. The ego is often horribly judgmental, and we pay a big price for it.

We insulate ourselves by building a box that keeps us separate from each other—but safe. At the same time, our true self longs to be expressed. It yearns for a sense of connection with others and relief from the endless concern with our fears and self-doubt. It's an amazing paradox that we are unknowingly guarding ourselves from the very thing that gives us the certainty and unshakable strength that we deeply long for. What's more, all that stands in the way of accessing this perspective is in-the-box thinking and our belief that it is not possible.

In-the-Box Thinking

Many feelings, thoughts, and responses are examples of in-the-box thinking. Here are a few you may recognize:

In-the-Box Thinking

Insecurities about yourself
Feelings of shame
Fear of being alone
Fear of being unlovable
Negative beliefs about yourself
Doubts about your abilities
Feeling overwhelmed or stuck in your life
Feeling resentful toward others
Worries about money
Negative beliefs about your body

It is important to realize that when you are experiencing these negative thoughts and feelings, it is only because you are in the box. They are not to be taken seriously, because the ego is not accurately appraising yourself or your life. These thoughts simply reflect the ego's perception of reality.

When we are in the box, we feel trapped, victimized, and powerless to change the way we feel or what we do. Our reactions feel like the only ones available. This perspective appears to be simply the way things *are,* and we seem relatively powerless to change it. The all-consuming nature of the box seems to override our ability to see alternate ways of responding. Take a few minutes to complete Exercise 1 and identify your most cherished in-the-box feelings.

Signs That You Are In the Box
Exercise 1

The first step in getting out of the box is to recognize that you are in it. Many thoughts and feelings are sure signs that you are in the box. For example, if you are feeling hopeless, fearful, anxious, or self-critical, it is pretty clear that you are in the box. These feelings in turn generate others: you may experience being stuck and unsure of yourself or your future. Think about being in the box and list those feelings and attitudes that accompany the experience.

In the Box

Examples:
1. Fear
2. Most of my anger
3. Worry
4. Self-doubt
5.
6.
7.
8.
9.
10.

Any and all limiting beliefs are a sign of being in the box. When we experience these beliefs, we feel trapped in an image of ourselves as unworthy and unable to do anything about our situation. But in truth, we are simply looking at ourselves, as well as others, through a dark lens that colors everything we see, think, and feel. There is truly no way out of this difficulty until we realize what we are doing. Once we do, we can correct our mistaken perceptions and respond more appropriately to any situation.

Try to identify the in-the-box thoughts, feelings, and actions in the following scenarios.

Mary and June were colleagues on the teaching staff of a private school in Vermont. While they never taught the same grades together, they did attend several of the same school functions and educational seminars. They didn't socialize outside of school, but they exchanged pleasantries about family and friends when they saw each other in the teachers' lounge or on the street. So it surprised Mary when she received a four-page tirade from June accusing her of being "a very self-absorbed individual" and as a coworker "not a giving or cooperative person." June went on to say, "Perhaps in your future interactions with others you might be more pleasant and friendlier. I no longer wish to communicate with you."

Mary felt extremely hurt and embarrassed for many months after receiving the letter, despite knowing that June had ended other relationships in a similar way. Rather than confront June, Mary chose to ignore her, and they didn't speak for the remainder of the year.

Although Mary's reactions to June's letter may seem "normal," it is important to identify the hurt and embarrassment she felt as an in-the-box reaction. While some psychothera-pists might have spoken to Mary about her lack of self-esteem, originating in her relationship with her critical mother, I would say that there is nothing wrong with Mary that an out-of-the-box tune-up can't fix.

June wrote a critical letter, and Mary was "trapped" in her emotional reaction. There seemed to be little choice for Mary but to respond as she did. That is being in the box. While it would be challenging for anyone to be judged so negatively and not feel hurt, angry, or resentful, there are other possible responses. One such out-of-the-box response would be for Mary to see that this might have more to do with June than with herself. Another response might be for Mary to examine whether she had actually been uncooperative with June and, if so, to acknowledge this to herself, learn from it, and move on. Thirdly, Mary could actually sit down with June and dis-cuss the situation face to face.

In the following chapters, you will learn ways to be free of automatic responses. For now, see how many in-the-box re-sponses you can glean from the story. Given the situation, what other in-the-box reactions, besides hurt and embarrass-ment, do you suspect Mary was feeling? Take a few minutes to identify them. How would you have reacted?

Clearly, June had her own set of in-the-box feelings and re-actions as well: She was resentful, condescending, angry, de-manding, and irrational. She justified her feelings by deciding she'd been victimized by Mary. June said in her letter that she was not open to discussion about her accusations, nor was she open to resolving them. She was both judge and jury. She personalized all kinds of encounters with Mary. Can you see how June's reactions and her inability to respond with care or compassion to what had occurred are results of being in the box?

Once we learn to spot our in-the-box reactions to difficult situations, we will know that there are alternative responses available, which we would never have thought of had we remained trapped in the tangled web of in-the-box emotions. By recognizing the feelings and thoughts that snare us, we'll discover a whole range of possibilities to free ourselves.

Remember, if you are experiencing any in-the-box feelings in a particular life situation, don't be hard on yourself. These feelings are not bad or wrong, they are just confining.

Now try this for yourself. See if you can find the in-the-box thoughts, feelings, and reactions in the following scenario. Look for the less apparent ones as well as the obvious ones.

Jack, an architect, got a call from a potential client who was interested in doing some major renovations on a house. The caller, Bernard, seemed impatient from the very beginning of the conversation. He wanted to know Jack's previous experience, his fee, a list of references, and his initial thoughts about how he would do the job. He also wanted to know when it would be completed, and he wanted the answers now.

Jack told him that he was more than willing to supply all the information but was up against a major deadline for another job. He asked Bernard if he could call him back in a couple of days, at which time he could give him his undivided attention. Bernard said that he had just a few more questions he needed to ask. Jack said he could spend two more minutes, but then he would have to go.

After another five questions, which took almost ten minutes, Jack said he had to get off the phone. Bernard responded by becoming very angry and hanging up on Jack. Jack was so upset by the phone call that it interfered with the quality of his work for the rest of the day.

Take a few minutes to consider the following question: what were the in-the-box reactions of both Jack and Bernard?

Bernard was being insensitive, aggressive, pushy, and demanding. He was not interested in Jack's dilemma. We have no idea what was going on with Bernard to cause him to act this way, and we don't need to know. His aggression and negativity were an indication that he was in the box.

Jack, on the other hand, was overwhelmed by work and frustrated at Bernard's lack of consideration. On top of everything else, he had to deal with the anger he felt after the conversation ended so abruptly. He also realized that by staying on the phone with Bernard, he had not taken care of his own needs. These are all in-the-box reactions.

As you can see, being in the box has many faces. Sometimes we blame our reactions on someone else, the situation, the weather, or the time of day. It doesn't matter as long as it's not us.

In-the-Box Beliefs and Feelings

Unless they are seen for what they are, any in-the-box beliefs and feelings render us seemingly powerless to change. They are like tentacles that encircle us and sap our faith in ourselves before we have time to realize what's happened. This is just where the ego wants us—mired in our feelings of hopelessness, discouragement, frustration, remorse, and blame. These feelings reflect our being in the box and keep us stuck thinking about what we do not want or do not have. They are certainly not empowering ways of being.

Exercise 2

Here a few familiar ones. See which ones you recognize, and think about the specific situations in which you use them. Then add your own.

In-the-Box Beliefs and Feelings

1. If only I were _____ [fill in the blank].
2. If only I had _____ [fill in the blank].
3. I should have _____ [fill in the blank].
4. I'm to blame for _____ [fill in the blank].
5. I'll never have enough_____ [fill in the blank] to be happy.
6.
7.
8.
9.
10.

You can feel the life being sucked right out of you as you ponder these familiar statements. They reflect an underlying sense of personal pain, shame, guilt, and regret. We may not even know why these feelings arise so easily in us, yet when they do, they are compelling and difficult to ignore or leave behind. We can be consumed by them. Despite the fact that there is generally little we can do about what has already happened, these irrational responses trap us in the past. It feels as if we have no choice. In order to make a different choice about how to respond, it is important to understand the ways in which we keep ourselves stuck.

How to Stay Stuck In the Box

If we were literally stuck in a box and could not get out, there is a good chance that we might ask ourselves, "Why did this have to happen to me?" Although it might be useful to know what we did to get stuck, most of the time we use that question to blame ourselves or someone else rather than to learn from our mistakes.

Similarly, when we're trapped in the metaphorical box of life, it is common to ask ourselves questions that keep us focused on what is wrong. The questions take many forms, but many will be quite familiar. For example, we often ask ourselves a question that has been, unfortunately, a large part of our culture and even of psychotherapeutic practice: What's wrong with me, and how did I get this way? The only possible answer to that question resides in our past, in something bad that has happened to us. It is not a question that moves us ahead in our lives or frees us from our concerns.

Imagine Mary asking herself a similar self-blaming question, such as "What is wrong with me that June treated me so badly?" Or "Why do people always treat me this way?" The answers to these questions point in one direction—discovering what is "wrong" with Mary and then figuring out how she got "damaged."

This is an approach championed by many therapists. Unfortunately, it keeps people believing that who they are is the sum total of what happened to them in the past. It also defines people by their problems, perpetuating the illusion that who we are and how we act are cast in stone. It can keep a client in therapy for many years.

If you want to find out what's wrong and what caused it, that's what you'll find—reasons for your problems, plus excuses for why you can't change. This is exactly what you want to *stop* doing. Once you get out of the box, that is the last thing you will spend your time focused on.

The best way to stop this endless cycle of searching for psychological causes and analyzing their effects is to have an alarm bell go off when you catch yourself asking certain questions that will keep you locked in the cycle. Here are some in-the-box questions that will certainly keep you trapped and not moving ahead. (Be sure to add some of your favorites.)

Exercise 3

In-the-Box Questions

1. Why do people always treat me so badly?
2. Why don't I ever get what I want?
3. What's wrong with me that I am so unhappy?
4. Why can't I meet the right person?
5. Why do I always sound so stupid?
6. What if I'm miserable the rest of my life? How will I cope?
7.
8.
9.
10.
11.

These questions do not focus our attention on moving forward, taking action, or looking for a new way of seeing things. They simply keep us focused on what is wrong.

The last way you keep yourself in the box is by repeating the same negative, upsetting conversations to yourself over and over again. Such repetition perpetuates the belief that things will never change and is basically a very annoying way to treat yourself. For example, June repeatedly worried about how people felt about her. These concerns were often in the forefront of her mind. Rather than trying to understand the origins of these insecurities (which most therapists would trace to her mother, father, sister, or brother), hoping that this understanding would change her thoughts, it might be more useful for June to recognize that insecurities are part of being human. Then she could learn how to access the place where these feelings become irrelevant and unimportant to her.

Like Mary, June, Bernard, and Jack, you certainly deserve a break from the habit of inflicting so much needless suffering on yourself and others. But first, it is important to understand how you perpetuate useless old beliefs and perspectives. See if you recognize any of the following types of internal monologue. Then add a few of your own.

Exercise 4

Perpetuating Old Beliefs and Perspectives

1. Focus your attention on things that upset you. For example, think about how embarrassed you feel about your appearance while you are trying to give an important presentation.

2. Don't update old beliefs and images of yourself, others, or the world. For example, see yourself as the same insecure, self-conscious person that you were as an adolescent.

3. Tell yourself hopeless things about your future, such as "I know I'll never be happy, no matter what I do."

4. Blame yourself for your past. For example, "It was probably my fault that I was abused by my spouse."

5.

6.

Perpetuating Old Beliefs and Perspectives (cont.)

7.

8.

9.

10.

The good news is that you are not the only one having these thoughts. Everyone's ego does the same thing, so it is nothing to take personally and nothing to pay much attention to. It is simply the background for all human experience, known as the human condition. Ultimately you will see these thoughts and feelings for what they are: reflections of an ego that is unable to perceive reality accurately because it is so consumed with fear about what might happen.

You will soon discover a clear distinction between how you respond to your in-the-box thoughts and feelings and how you respond to the very same thoughts and feelings from out of the box. Quite simply, from in the box, emotional reactions aren't questioned, you merely respond to them. From out of the box, you see how mistaken and irrelevant they are to the life you want to live. Insecurities, doubts, and fears, all restrict your enjoyment of life. When you understand this and choose to do something about it, your unquestioned allegiance to this voice in your head begins to waver. A possibility arises for a new beacon to guide your responses to life. Your faith is placed in what truly honors you, and that makes a profound difference in how you live.

It is vitally important to identify when we are being taken

hostage by our ego and are accepting the criticism and torment that it inflicts on us. When we stop this madness in ourselves, we also begin to end this predicament on the planet. We will have broken through our conditioning and, in doing so, increased the chances that others will be able to follow in our footsteps.

Remember, the ego's main purpose is to provide protection from the outside world and to keep things as they have always been. It is basically unwilling to yield its power and control. It simply won't do so on its own. Despite the fact that the ego is making our life miserable with its unending barrage of doubts, worries, negativity, and fear, at least this perspective is familiar. The way we react today will be much the same as the way we've reacted for decades. This, to the ego, is a job well done. The feelings and reactions that cause us a great deal of pain are at least predictable, practiced, and safe. Accepting this predicament is the way the ego reigns supreme over our life. But we *can* take back control if we choose to, by circumventing the ego with the processes described in the next three chapters.

3

Getting Out of the Box

Once you know with absolute certainty that nothing can trouble you but your own imagination, you come to disregard your desires and fears, concepts and ideas, and live by truth alone. . . .

Instead of searching for what you do not have, find out what it is that you have never lost.
— Sri Nisargadatta Maharaj, *I Am That*

Out-of-the-Box Thinking

What if being free is just a choice? What if getting out of the box is a metaphor for being free? Free from our self-imposed limitations, doubts, and fears. Free to choose how we want to feel, what we want to think, and how we want to live our life. Free to act in ways that enhance our sense of self and promote a sense of well-being.

This chapter will show you how to make this choice. It will then give you the necessary tools for living from the choice you have made.

Getting Out of the Box

Imagine that after being stuck in the box and almost giving up believing that you would ever get out, you found that you were able to cut a hole in the side of the box and climb out. You are now free, and your *mind* is free. You may sense a feeling of relief, liberation, or joy. It may be like other moments in your life when you felt this sense of freedom and possibility.

When I want to get out of the box, I recall how life looks to me when I am experiencing and knowing from this perspective. The musings of my ego become completely irrelevant. Instead I focus some of my attention on being free—unwilling to give it up for anything—and the rest of my attention on whatever I am involved with. Then the commitment to being free becomes the context through which I see the world. I do not let my attention waiver one inch from my commitment to being free in this moment. Spiritual teachers have described this kind of attention as having one eye focused within and one eye focused out. (But please do not think the eye focused within means that you are focused on the thoughts of the ego. It certainly does not. The eye within is focused purely on being free.)

As you look around from out of the box, what do you see? How do you feel? What is your sense of being alive? How does your life look to you now? What are you doing? Carefully notice how it feels to be suddenly and totally free. Take a few moments to fully experience being free.

This experience will be most helpful as you choose to get out of the box in the future.

This is how it feels when we are not experiencing life through the distortion of the ego. It is real and true. It is a perspective that will get deeper and more profound as its implications and uses become more apparent.

From this new perspective, we might feel a sense of well-being, happiness, confidence, hope, strength, lightness, or a feeling of being fully alive, spontaneous, and free. We might also feel something quite different from what I have described. That's fine, as long as it embodies the essence of freedom.

When you first experience being out of the box, you may feel some discomfort with your newfound freedom. The ego may tell you that what you are experiencing is not real, not you, not what you need, and not important anyway. If the ego says these things and you agree, recognize it as a symptom of still being in the box and being too interested in what the ego has to say. It is the ego's way of holding on by taking the simple state of feeling free and making it into a problem. This is the way the ego usually responds when confronted with a new possibility. It tells us to be afraid and to turn back.

In fact, some people, when asked how it feels to be trapped in a dark airless box where they can't even move, say that it feels *good*. This is the ego hanging on for dear life. It almost sounds as if they like it so much they're about to start decorating. This is a sure sign that they are being pinned down by their own fears. It may also be a sign that they feel so overwhelmed by choices and responsibilities in their life that having *no* options is comforting.

Pam was exhausted after returning home from her second trip to her firm's West Coast office in the same week, where she had been asked to give yet another presentation to the management team. When I asked her to imagine being in the box, she said it was such a relief to be alone in there with no responsibilities that she wanted to lock the door and throw away the key.

We can all relate to that in-the-box feeling of being completely overwhelmed by life.

To the ego, being out of the box may feel like too much responsibility. So the ego tells us that we cannot handle it and that we don't really want it in the first place. The ego will tell us that it can take care of us just fine without this "freedom stuff." This shows us that it is still unwilling to let us go and also reveals how it tries to obstruct our progress by keeping our thinking in the box. The difference is that now we don't have to listen. We no longer have to stay trapped in the box. We know how to get free. We do not need to be fooled by the mind's tricks. Just keep going, and don't stop until you experience being free.

If your ego is holding on in any way, my suggestion is that you not judge yourself. Be patient. Simply take some more time until you are definitely out of the box. Breathe, lighten up, and enjoy the process of getting your life back in your hands.

In the box and *out of the box* describe opposite ends of the spectrum of how life can be lived. They are mutually exclusive. We are either in the box or out. Being in the box implies that we are trapped by something beyond our control that is causing us pain. The feelings may include being stuck, worried, anxious, frustrated, lonely, betrayed, or angry at our predicament. Whatever the feelings or their circumstances, we feel powerless to change either the cause or its effect on us.

This is in stark contrast to being out of the box. From this wonderful place, we have options and are literally able to move freely. The world is no longer imposing itself on us, and we no longer feel limited. We have choices. This alone is a very significant factor in how we feel and respond to the world. Feeling free to move is contagious; you'll soon feel free to choose how you want to respond to all aspects of your life. You can respond as a slave of your ego or as a person of free will. Choose one.

A client who had felt victimized by circumstances throughout his life called me from Virginia to ask for help. During our first telephone session, Mark, twenty-six years old, single, very bright, articulate, and determined, spoke of his passion for becoming an opera singer. He faced many obstacles and wondered whether it was a "realistic dream."

As a young boy he had been diagnosed with Tourette's syndrome, a neurological disorder that results in involuntary movements of the body (such as tics) and involuntary vocal expressions (such as curse words). Because of this, he was regularly ostracized and humiliated by his schoolmates. His family was ashamed and embarrassed by his symptoms and was not particularly supportive or loving. Beginning at age eleven, Mark was forced to go to a very controlling and unhelpful therapist whom he saw for almost a decade. He was placed on heavy medication at a young age to limit his symptoms, which made him feel dull and numb (he described the feeling as being "chemically lobotomized"). Several years ago, he had found a holistic physician in New York City who successfully took him off these medications.

He contacted me because he had to decide by the end of the week whether to stay in Virginia or move to California to take opera classes. Although he was terrified by the thought of the move, he said, "I have to sing opera. I know it's what I was put here for." He wondered whether he should instead become a physician (a career that was not really very interesting to him but that his parents thought he should pursue) or be a cantor at the local synagogue, where he had sung before (a choice that was clearly not his passion). He was feeling pulled in different directions by friends and family and felt he was being asked to abandon his dream.

I led Mark through the process of getting out of the box, and he was easily able to experience the freedom of this state. I asked him if there were other times in his life when *he had experienced a similar feeling. He said that it was much like the feeling he had whenever he sang, which was like "talking to God." That was all I needed to hear. His insecurities and doubts were about to take a walk.*

I asked Mark to hold onto that feeling and to simultaneously think of being an opera singer. He joyfully said, "I feel extremely free." As we talked about the expectations of others, he said that from this perspective, "Nothing can touch me. I can't help but realize who I am. I'm an entirely different person when I am in the box. That's the key. It's incredible!" When I asked him how his fears appeared to him, he said, "I wouldn't have any, and if I did, I wouldn't pay any attention to them!"

We spoke about how he could return to this perspective at any time: it was who he really was, and it was real. We also spoke about how, from this perspective, he must do his life's work: it was all he really wanted.

He called the next day and told me that he had been with his friends and family and that for the first time they were actually being much more supportive of him. "All day I felt free and easy and happy. I feel very different. It's such an incredible difference! Nothing can possibly bother me from here." He realized that "It's not about where I live. It's about me." All that mattered, he said, was that he realized his dream.

This perspective will reveal to you, as it did to Mark, what makes your heart sing, and you will do all you can to honor it. You will not just hope, you will act. There is nothing else to do. Your reasons for not doing so will disappear, and you will see the path to your fulfillment. There are many other gifts that this perspective will offer, but finding your heart's desire is one of the most rewarding.

Once you have experienced being out of the box yourself, you can begin to recognize the thoughts and feelings that accompany this perspective. As you do, you will be able to distinguish between feelings and actions that are in the box and those that are out of the box. Here are some examples.

In the Box	Out of the Box
Feeling insecure	Feeling confident
Judging or resenting	Accepting or understanding
Feeling overwhelmed or tired	Taking action or becoming unstuck
Feeling negative	Feeling hopeful or positive

Which would you rather be: insecure, fretful, and pessimistic or confident, forward-thinking, and hopeful?

When we climb free of the walls that imprison us, life changes in a profound way. We become open, liberated, happy, at peace, in charge, unburdened, and able to move. Choosing this vast new perspective has extraordinary implications for all aspects of our life.

Signs That You Are Out of the Box
Exercise 5

If you are feeling a sense of freedom, possibility, hope, or joy or if you are taking steps that are moving you ahead in your life, you are probably out of the box. Take a few minutes to compile your own description of this state. You might ask yourself, "If I were out of the box right now, how would I feel? How would I see life?" Then list those feelings and attitudes.

EXAMPLES

1. A sense of freedom
2. A feeling of compassion toward others
3. A feeling of confidence
4. A sense of wonder about life
5. Taking action in the face of fear
6.

7.

8.

9.

10.

Add your descriptions, and tuck a copy in your wallet or purse. Having this list available at challenging times will remind you exactly how you felt when you were "clear." It will also be a beacon to guide you back when you feel yourself slipping into the darkness of the box.

Who You Are

My one hope for the way this book could most deeply affect us, and for humankind as well, is that we would finally realize that our true humanity is lying just below the surface, waiting to be set free. It is up to us to recognize it, accept it, release it, and express it. When we recognize that this place inside is always available and is our deepest expression, it becomes our responsibility, not only to ourselves but more importantly to each other, to live from this realization. It is not only our birthright, it is our imperative, to do what we can to bring about a transformation on the planet. When we choose to end the suffering *within ourselves*, we are doing all we can to change the course of evolution. There can be no greater legacy to leave behind.

We do not need to be a particular type of person to succeed with this process. Getting out of the box is dependent only on our desire to be free of our suffering and our willingness to see life anew. Sometimes it will take a powerful commitment to be free, and great courage in the face of the ego's need for control. At these times, remember this: all the ego offers us is more pain and suffering. What it wants is our aliveness, spontaneity, and sense of well-being. Succumb to it and we ultimately give up our chance for a profoundly satisfying life. If instead we begin to listen to the innate wisdom of our true self, the source of the ego's power over us will disappear. The game then becomes interesting.

In order to make the transition from the choppy waters of the limiting mind to the calm seas of our true self, I am suggesting a four-step approach. This will be the foundation upon which all else rests.

Four Steps to Getting Out of the Box: Expanded Approach for the Most Challenging Times

There are times when getting out of the box will be as simple as asking "If I were out of the box right now, how would I feel? What would I do? What would I be thinking about?" At other times—for instance when we are in the middle of an emotional upset—it will be more challenging. The challenge stems from our intense identification with our emotional state, especially with what upsets us. We all know how oppressive our fear, anger, jealousy, and worry can be.

In order to resolve an upset, we must make the choice to do so—and look at it from another perspective. The quickest, easiest way to do this is to put our upset on a shelf until we get out of the box and have the resources to see it clearly. But how, in the midst of confusion and pain, can we do that?

The *four-step process* offers a useful way back from emotional turmoil. To understand the approach, consider the following scenario of a husband, Jeff, and wife, Julia, who came to see me for marital counseling. Each used the process in their own way to resolve an upset they had in their relationship. We will look at how each one effectively handled the situation, first from the husband's point of view and then from the wife's.

Jeff said that when he came home from work one evening, his wife of ten years angrily told him that he was not doing enough around the house and yelled in his face that she was "not cooking dinner tonight!" She went up to the bedroom and slammed the door. Jeff did not know what she was so angry about, whether it was something he'd done or something that had happened at work. Either way, he did not feel he deserved such treatment and felt his own anger and frustration rising to the surface.

Here's how Jeff used the four steps to resolve the situation.

STEP 1: RECOGNIZE THAT YOU'RE IN THE BOX.

As we've seen, an in-the-box state of mind is when we feel confined by four solid walls, a floor, and a low ceiling. The box is bleak, empty, and confining. We may feel trapped, claustrophobic, and scared. Recall the emotional signs that we are stuck in the box: for example, fear, worry, hopelessness, anxiety, isolation, self-doubt, self-blame, self-criticism, and anger. It's the ego that is causing these feelings and making us suffer so much.

The sense of limitation, constriction, and pain you are feeling is nothing more than evidence that you are in the box. Whenever you feel any of these in-the-box feelings, it's time to get out. Remember, the difficulty is not the situation you confront but the way you choose to perceive it. There is a vast difference between the way a "problem" looks from in the box and out of the box.

The ego will never give us a wake-up call. *We* must be the one to realize what's happening. Once we recognize that we're in the box, we can do something about it, but not before.

Jeff immediately knew that his anger and frustration were evidence that he was in the box. He was reacting to what Julia had said and taking it personally. He may not have wanted to react this way, but it was an automatic response, which he was very familiar with. This time Jeff knew that he did not have to remain trapped in his emotional response. He could make a choice to respond in a new way that gave him what he wanted—resolution and harmony—rather than what his ego was so enamored with—anger, separation, and pain. Jeff's awareness that his reaction was in the box fueled his desire to take the next step.

STEP 2: PUT THE ISSUE ASIDE.

We can't focus simultaneously on what is upsetting us *and* on getting out of the box, because we can't be in and out of the box at the same time. It's just not possible. So, imagine putting the issue that is concerning you on a shelf. Just put it there for safekeeping until you're ready to look at it again. This will free you to focus entirely on making the shift necessary to get out of the box. The key is to focus on being free rather than on your pain.

It is very difficult to gain clarity and objectivity when we are in the middle of an upset. But our clearest insight into what happened and why we responded the way we did will come only when we are out of the box. We don't need to do anything about the issue right now. We can come back to it when we are thinking more clearly.

By shelving the issue until he got out of the box, Jeff stopped focusing on his upset. This gave him the space he needed to see the situation with greater clarity. He did not have to re-solve the issue, he just had to put it on hold until he could free himself from the emotionally challenged ego. Doing this pre-pared him for the next step, which was to get out of the box.

STEP 3: ASK AND ANSWER QUESTIONS TO GET OUT OF THE BOX.

Because the issue is still on the shelf, we can focus our at-tention on asking questions in a way that immediately frees us from the ego and provides an entirely new outlook on who we have considered ourselves to be and on life itself. There are many variations of these questions that can be used, and I will say much more about this in Chapter Five, but for now, the most neutral questions that allow the issue to remain on the shelf while still forwarding our intention to get out of the box are:

If I were out of the box right now, what would I be experi-encing?

How would I be feeling?
What would I be doing?
What would I be thinking?

When you ask these questions, you begin to move through any barriers you might believe are in the way and enter onto the path that will lead you out of the box. By answering the questions, you allow yourself to experience the state of being out of the box, or being free from the ego.

Jeff's answers to the questions were "I would be thinking that being out of the box was the most important thing to me right now, and I am not giving it up for anything. This is my priority. I know that everything else that I really want in my life will stem from this. I have a choice about how I respond to whatever occurs in my life, and my choice is to honor this sense of freedom no matter what it takes. From here, I feel my commitment to Julia, and I know that regardless of what is going on with her or with us, we will work it out."

The solutions for any situation you are trying to resolve come easily from the powerful yet compassionate stance that arises when you answer the "What if I were out of the box now?" questions. They are right in front of you, and you can trust them. All there is to do is to act on what you realize to be true. Then you are giving yourself the most extraordinary gift you can, a profound connection to your true heart and to the true source of your wisdom and love. It is quite thrilling to experience yourself in this way, and as long as you fully choose to stay there, *nothing* can take you away from that place within, it's so powerful and compelling.

The out-of-the-box questions and answers will help you quickly shift your perspective in any situation. But if that doesn't happen so easily at first, it really doesn't matter. I promise that you'll be able to shift it, as long as you don't stop until you are out of the box. At those times when the emotions are more difficult (as when your spouse has just gotten angry at you), you can turn your attention to trusting that this perspective awaits you. After putting your feelings on a shelf, you can ask yourself the questions to get free. Then be sensitive to the slightest sensation that lets you know the heaviness is lifting and your thoughts are starting to change. Stay with it until you are free.

Simply remember to maintain a one-pointed focus: I want to

be out of the box more than anything else right now. That determination will give you what you need to shift your perspective. When you do this you will succeed, as long as you do not give in to the tempting belief that it is too difficult to do.

The ego will tell you how hard it is in many disguised ways. In regard to getting out of the box, it may say something like "Why try? It's just too much trouble right now." Or "You have a right to be angry and upset for as long as you want." Jeff's ego probably said something like "The heck with her. She yelled at me for no reason. She should come to me and apologize first. It's her fault that I'm upset now!" The work will be to recognize and then disregard the voice of the ego, which will try to insinuate itself back into your life. It wants you trapped in your emotional upsets because then you are back in its hands, where it can do with you as it wishes. In the next chapter, these and other ego tricks will be revealed for what they are, and you'll learn to circumvent them.

When you do recognize the ego at work, you can simply ask yourself the question "If I were out of the box now, what would I think about the justification for my anger and cynicism?" The answer is that "I would pay little attention to it because I would be focused on something far more important: resolving my upset as quickly as possible, learning from it, moving on, and being free again." When you are responding to your questions in this manner and working toward a resolution, you are officially out of the box.

STEP 4: NOW THAT YOU ARE OUT OF THE BOX, LOOK AT THE
ISSUE THAT WAS TROUBLING YOU.

Once Jeff asked and answered his own questions to get out of the box, he could again focus his attention on his commitment to Julia and to himself. After all, this is what he truly wanted. Although his ego may have wanted him to retaliate for Julia's unkind statement, to feel like a victim, or to feel justified in pulling further apart, this is not what Jeff's true self wanted. As you may have surmised, the true self is not a big fan of pain, separation, constriction, and anger.

Now that he was out of the box, Jeff could take the issue off the shelf with the knowledge that he was looking at it from a clear place. That clarity allowed him to respond to Julia very differently: "I know that things have really been tough for you lately, but I really don't deserve to be spoken to like this. Is there some other way you can deal with your anger rather than taking it out on me? Is there something that you need? If you ever don't want to cook dinner, just tell me, and we'll go out to eat. If you're feeling overwhelmed with anything, or want to talk, please tell me. I really love you, but I am not willing to have you take your upsets out on me. I really do get hurt by it. So I would appreciate it if you would talk to me about what you are feeling or ask me for what you need instead."

Jeff's response was clearly loving, respectful, and out of the box. It consisted of an offer to help and a natural compassion for Julia while honoring his own needs and requests for change. He no longer took Julia's anger personally, nor did he fight back. He said how he felt without blame. Neither the box nor the ego was distorting his reality. His true self was in charge, and he was free.

This is Julia's version of what happened and how she responded.

Julia explained that while she was at work, her mother had called to say that she expected Julia and the children to come spend the day with her on Saturday. Julia had already made plans weeks before to take some much needed time for herself. She had set up play dates for both of the children and made an appointment for a day at a spa. She was torn between pleasing her mother and taking care of herself. By taking care of her mother, her own needs would be compromised. It made her very angry. At the height of her anger, Jeff came home from work and said, "Hi, honey, what's for dinner? I'm starved." Before she knew what was happening, she heard herself yelling, "I'm not cooking dinner tonight! And why don't you do more around the house?" Then she turned on her heel, went to the bedroom, and slammed the door.

Julia used the out-of-the-box process to resolve her feelings about the stresses in her life and the upsets with Jeff and her mother.

STEP 1: JULIA RECOGNIZED THAT SHE WAS IN THE BOX.

Julia realized that the frustration and anger she had directed toward Jeff was a signal that she was in the box. Although she felt overwhelmed by all the responsibilities she had at work and at home, she knew that Jeff hadn't really done anything wrong. If anyone were responsible for what happened, it was her mother and herself. She did not want to be angry at Jeff, although she did think that changes needed to be made regarding how their domestic responsibilities were divided. She believed that with clarity (which she knew she lacked at that moment) she could maturely discuss the situation. She recognized that the primary obstacle to resolving these issues was her feeling trapped in her emotional reaction. She was in the box.

STEP 2: SHE PUT THE ISSUE ASIDE.

In order to get out of the box, there were several issues Julia had to put on the shelf: anger at her mother's demands and her own inability to say no; feeling torn between wanting to please her mother and needing to take time for herself; disappointment over the possibility of missing a day of pampering; and frustration about Jeff's limited responsibilities at home. She hoped the shelf was securely fastened, because this was a heavy load to bear.

Despite the onslaught of feelings, she knew that it was best to approach the issues with clarity, so she imagined that she had put all of them on a shelf in the basement closet and locked the door. She wanted to get as far away from them as she could. This was all she needed to do with them right now.

STEP 3: SHE ASKED HERSELF QUESTIONS AND FOUND THE
ANSWERS TO GET HERSELF OUT OF THE BOX.

The answers to Julia's questions lay in the knowledge that she needed to be compassionate with herself and take care of herself as well as others in her life. Like Jeff, she asked herself "If I were out of the box right now, how would I be feeling? What would I be thinking about? What would I be doing?"

She said that she felt at ease, untroubled, and energized. She thought, "I can create the kind of life I want to have. There's time and energy for me to do everything I want with my family and for myself. In reality, my life is good, and I should feel blessed." She came to the conclusion that she would do whatever was necessary to begin each day as if it were full of possibility and to honor those she cared most about with compassion and respect.

Once she answered the questions, she immediately discovered a renewed sense of passion for life, an appreciation for all that she had, and a sense that anything was possible. By asking and answering these questions she was led back home to her true self.

The issues that had gripped her moments before were seen as reminders of how far astray her ego had taken her from what she knew she wanted and who she was. Now she was ready to look again at what had happened with eyes that could see clearly and would never deceive her.

STEP 4: NOW THAT JULIA WAS OUT OF THE BOX, SHE COULD LOOK AT THE ISSUES THAT WERE TROUBLING HER.

This newfound clarity opened the door to Julia's wisdom and understanding. She could now see what had really happened and how to resolve it. From out of the box she knew that taking time for herself every week was absolutely imperative for her well-being as well as the family's. She planned to call a family meeting with Jeff and the children to discuss how they would divide certain household chores so that she was not responsible for everything.

As for her mother, Julia realized that she needed to count on some quality time with Julia and the grandchildren. She intended to sit down with her mother to plan an interesting, fun day trip once a month. They would include the children in the planning so that everyone would get to choose an activity they would enjoy. It would give her mother something to look forward to. It would also help to alleviate her mother's tendency to "demand" time with Julia and the children. As well, Julia would not feel the guilt of having to say no when the timing did not work well. She was thrilled with the possibility of being able to take care of her mother without compromising herself and having some fun with her children to boot. Everyone seemed to win with this plan (which they did).

In regard to Jeff, Julia realized that she did not want to take her anger out on the person she loved most. She knew that Jeff would do anything for her. All she had to do was ask.

While she felt that Jeff needed to take more responsibility around the house, yelling at him was not the way to accomplish it. Julia needed to find a way to express her upset and take responsibility for her feelings. From out of the box, she realized that anger and yelling were just the ego's way of keeping her from having what she truly wanted. She wanted a happy, loving, healthy, productive life with satisfying relationships. From this new perspective she knew exactly how to get it.

It is easy to see how two people can be so close and yet so far away in their lives together. To become true partners again, all it takes is a simple shift in our priorities. Then the questions become "Would you rather be right or be close? Would you rather be angry or loving? Would you rather take care of others at the expense of yourself or honor your needs as well?" From out of the box, the issues and conflicts of everyday life are easily workable, and the process of resolving them can be amazingly satisfying.

Jeff and Julia realized that with clarity, conviction, and commitment, they were able to resolve their differences in a way that brought them closer than ever before. The differences were no longer sources of discord but were ways to deepen their understanding of each other's needs.

Once we are free and can breathe life in again, we have a whole new lens through which to see the issues that are troubling us. This is definitely the best vantage point from which to solve problems, because our wisdom is now available to us. Where before we may have felt trapped in anger and resentment, now we can choose how we want to respond to what has happened. Our touchstone will be wanting to be free.

From this new perspective you will see your issues or concerns in a very different light. Here's how they'll look:

If You Were . . .	Are You Now . . .
Angry	Compassionate
Anxious	Calm
In despair	Hopeful
Frightened	Relieved
Feeling trapped	Feeling free
Stuck or confused	Seeing options or moving ahead
Helpless	Empowered
Worried	Taking action

Focus on the following three important reminders:

1. This perspective is already there waiting to be found.

The out-of-the-box perspective is already and always waiting for us, no matter how far away it may appear or how impossible finding it may seem. When we stop listening to that negative inner voice, we will be justly rewarded. I am not exaggerating when I say that it is a thrill when we get to the other side of an issue and see how unnecessary our upset actually was.

2. Don't stop until you get there!

The ego will try many ways to dissuade us from getting out of the box. Don't listen. Don't be swayed by it. Don't honor it in any way. If we persevere, we can overcome the ego's desire to stay with pain, anger, and hurt. This means that we must counter the ego's strong desire to stay stuck with an equally strong force: our desire to get unstuck. Don't be afraid to work hard at this. It may save time at very difficult moments in your life, such as when you are angry at your friend for forgetting to call or when your husband or wife is an hour late. This is not to say that you *should* get out of the box whenever something is bothering you. It is to say that if you choose to do so, you always *can*. The choice is yours.

From this perspective we can also see that it is important to take time to heal from painful situations in our lives, such as when a loved one dies or an intimate relationship ends. Taking time to heal is absolutely necessary, and from out of the box we would be committed to doing so. But we can often begin to resolve our upsets much more quickly than we usually do with the clarity we find from this new perspective. We just don't linger in the pain because there is no reason to.

3. Be compassionate with yourself.

When we are in the box, we often judge, blame, and criticize ourselves for all sorts of things. That's what the ego does. It makes us believe there is something wrong with us, and we focus on it like a laser. It is almost "natural" to call ourselves stupid when we make even the smallest mistake. The ego just never gives us a break. It's not surprising, then, that we often treat others with the same lack of compassion.

So it is especially important at challenging times that we make the choice to treat ourselves, as well as others, with deep compassion, respect, and caring. We know that once we are out of the box, that is what we would do.

Who's Driving This Train, Anyway?

One of the greatest rewards of being out of the box is that we are no longer at the mercy of our in-the-box thinking. We see it for what it is, and we simply ignore what it has to say. With time this new response becomes almost automatic, especially at less challenging times in our life.

From in the box our thoughts mean everything. If we think, "I'll never be successful at that job, why even try?" we probably won't try anything new or different. From out of the box, that same thought (and we will still have them) might be met with the response "If I really want that job, I'm going after it. It's the only way I will ever know if I could have been successful or not. If I give it everything I've got, then I'll know for sure what I am capable of. That's the only way to find out."

The out-of-the-box perspective is not one that views every challenge as appropriate to undertake for its own sake. It simply opens the space for us to choose with rationality and with a passionate desire to know what is right and true.

When you hear the ego tell you "No. Don't try. Give up. Accept what you have. Forget it," you will immediately reject such thoughts. Rather than responding to its fear, doubt, insecurity, and shame, you will respond from what is truly in your best interests. Remember, your ego will keep cranking out those old messages, like an assembly line. That is what it does, it is so insecure and frightened. But you will learn to see those thoughts as creations of that machinery rather than as creations of your true self. You will observe them rather than embrace them. You will simply leave those thoughts alone.

You've got other things to think about—like being free, happy, and secure within yourself. Where before those thoughts were the primary obstacle to your happiness, they are now seen as empty reminders of bygone days. You will naturally have the tools, the ability, and the will to move ahead, and you will do just that. Nothing less will suffice.

How Do You Get to Carnegie Hall?

Getting out of the box gets easier, more familiar, and more a part of who we are with practice. For this reason I often ask clients to list, eight to ten times a week, how they have gotten out of the box. Doing this regularly helps to keep us aware of the technique and reminds us to use it. It also helps us to recognize the issues that are most challenging for us. Being successful also builds confidence that even at difficult times, we can always get out of the box.

The next exercise will help you keep track of your progress.

How I Got Out of the Box
Exercise 6

For the next two weeks, keep a running record of your daily out-of-the-box experiences. List at least two times you got out of the box each day. In a few sentences, describe the situation that was getting you stuck and what you did to get out. Then describe how different the situation looked after you got out of the box. The example here is somewhat longer than what you need to do, but the added detail may give you an idea of the format to use.

When I came into the office this morning, my boss, Steve, angrily returned a report I'd given up my weekend to write, saying that it needed a lot of work. I felt ashamed, angry, and hurt. I wanted to quit on the spot. What does he want from me? I'm giving this job everything I've got.

In order to free myself from these in-the-box reactions, I decided first to put my feelings aside. Then I asked myself, "What if I were out of the box right now? How would I feel, what would I do, how would I respond?"

I realized from this perspective that there was nothing to be ashamed of. I had simply made some mistakes, and I could correct them. I remembered how much I really liked my work before this happened. I then decided to rewrite the report, acknowledging Steve's comments and criticisms, and resubmit it. In the end I learned from the experience and was absolutely fine!

Take the time to congratulate yourself each time you make this important choice to be free.

Getting In the Box and Getting Back Out

Now think of a challenging issue in your life. Look at it from out of the box, and then look at it from back inside. How different is your response? Do you see how ridiculous it is to *choose* to feel bad and *choose* to be stuck when there is another way?

While it may sound counterproductive, another way to practice getting out of the box is to practice getting in. This takes some degree of trust in your ability to get out and trust that this perspective is *always* there waiting for you, no matter how you feel at any particular moment. This is a very empowering exercise. I suggest that people do it to strengthen their muscles, reaffirm their ability, and deepen their commitment to this perspective. When you are not afraid of getting back in the box because you know that you can get right back out, you are proving to yourself that you are not your in-the-box thoughts. This is crucial to understand.

Instant exercise:

First get out of the box in the usual way. Then ask questions to firmly entrench yourself in the box, such as "If I were *in* the box right now, how would I feel? What would I be thinking about? What would I be doing? How negative would I feel? How insecure would I be? How bad would life look?"

Once you are definitely back in the box (and these questions should get you there just fine), then ask yourself the out-of-the-box questions to get back out again. Try this a few times. It's amazing how this exercise builds confidence in your ability to get free. You realize that you do not have to worry about getting in the box because you can always get back out. You see exactly how you have regularly and unknowingly put yourself in. Conversely, you see how quickly you can shift your perspective to get back out, and its profound effect on you.

Spontaneous Moments of Freedom

This is how a human being can change:
There's a worm addicted to eating grape leaves.
Suddenly he wakes up, call it grace, whatever,
     something wakes him, and he's no longer a worm.
He's the entire vineyard,
And the orchard too, the fruit, the trunks,
a growing wisdom and joy that doesn't need to devour.
     —JELALUDDIN RUMI, FROM *THE WORM'S WAKING*

Many people have had spontaneous spiritual experiences. These states might alternatively be described as mystical, enlightened, free, out of the box, or in the zone.

During a conference in 1981 on the subject of "Mastery in Psychotherapy" led by my mentor Dr. Bob Shaw, I awoke one morning in a state I could only describe as pure ecstasy and possibility. I was flying! Everything was possible. I called Bob in his hotel room at about 7:30 A.M. and told him that I wanted to lead the class. He knew what I was experiencing, and he happily said he would think about it.

I was later invited to the front of the room to address the other therapists. I will never forget the experience and the look on the faces of several colleagues who were literally crying tears of joy as they listened to me express such a state of ecstasy, passion, confidence, and freedom. I was completely free of all self-consciousness, I was so deeply in touch with what was possible for us all, and that was all I cared about and all I wanted to express. It was an extraordinary moment in my life that still reminds me of who I really am and how life actually is. I continue to draw upon that understanding. Many similar experiences were to follow, which revealed a great deal that eventually formed the foundation of this approach.

It is useful to recall these experiences if you have had them and to recognize that these moments offer a glimpse into what life can be and who you are. We usually do not interpret these experiences in that way. We see them as something that "just happened to us" and was therefore out of our control. We feel lucky to have had them and want them to happen again, but we haven't known how to bring it about. We can now see that these moments can be recreated. It is important to recall these experiences for the insight they gave us into ourselves. It is important to accept them as real and true.

Spontaneous Out-of-the Box Moments
Exercise 7

Recall a time in your life when you were spontaneously out of the box. You may have felt a sense of profound freedom, a sense that "you" were not there, or a feeling of joy and wonder at life itself. These moments may have occurred when you were in awe of nature, dancing, experiencing the beauty of a magnificent piece of artwork, when you were skiing or running, or when you were making love. You might have experienced being without your usual burdens, concerns, or sense of separateness from others or from life itself. At these moments, clients have described to me a sense of oneness with the world, the presence of God, pure joy, and being absolutely at peace within themselves.

Take a moment to recall one or more of these special moments. Then answer the following questions:

How did I feel? What was my experience of being alive?

Do these moments have anything in common in terms of how I was responding or what I was doing?

What can I learn about life from the perspective these experiences gave me?

How can I use this perspective?

Can I recreate the feeling now? What does it reveal?

Am I willing to accept what I experienced at these moments as insight into my true nature and the way life really is and could be for me?

My wife had one particular life experience that she would describe as being spontaneously out of the box.

Several years ago while white-water rafting in the Grand Canyon, she spent a day hiking out from the riverbed to the wide open plains above the canyon walls. Just as the sun was setting she began walking up large land-steps and felt as if she was on the "stairway to heaven." The sky changed from blue to raspberry, purple, and gold. She remembers feeling full of love, color, and God. She often draws on this memory to get back into her heart or remember that life can be magical.

Many people find it useful to recall the times when they spontaneously found themselves out of the box. Such memories are a perfect road map back to this perspective. To partake of the richness of this experience, ask yourself, "What if I were seeing life from this perspective right now? What does it reveal to me? What does it reveal about myself?"

By recalling and drawing upon these experiences, you will

be reminded of what is possible, and you will have begun to embody its lessons about life. So do take the time to recall the most poignant, memorable, or profound moments in your life when you sensed this freedom and try to understand the experience as deeply as you can. Remember how your body felt, how life looked to you, and how you felt about yourself. Trust that this was a window into your soul and into the way life can truly be.

A Path of Action and Solutions

Once we can see life from a viewpoint that is undistorted by the doubts, fears, and worries of the ego and not mired in emotional upsets, what magically appears before us is a clear path of action. At that moment, our attention shifts totally to finding the way to have what we want. Fears become meaningless because our focus is on achieving our goal, moving ahead, or making desired changes in our life. From this new perspective, we can direct our focus in a positive rather than a negative or fear-filled direction. We are released from the burdens of worry and insecurity.

Margaret, a third-year medical student who is successfully overcoming a serious cancer, felt shaken to her core by the fear of becoming homeless. She had no money whatsoever to pay current medical and housing bills. Her school loans totaled $200,000 and would become due if she dropped out or flunked out. Her parents had died, she had no siblings, and she had no one to ask for money. From in the box, she felt completely overwhelmed and powerless about her situation.

Although most people would agree that her situation was incredibly challenging, it did not mean that paralysis was the only possible reaction. As she described what was going on, I expressed my concern for her difficult situation. We then discussed how her fear and paralysis were in-the-box attitudes, which reflected a limited and powerless view. Rather than focusing on how overwhelming it all was, she needed to put her concerns on the shelf and devise a definite plan to get some money.

Margaret began by asking herself, "If I were out of the box right now, where could I borrow money?" The only possibility was her frugal but well-heeled Aunt Helen. Even though Helen had refused financial help in the past, Margaret decided that she would no longer accept no for an answer.

In the box, she felt too embarrassed to ask and feared rejection. From the out-of-the-box perspective, her worries disappeared because the primary concern of surviving, and reducing the stress on her body became paramount. She agreed to write her aunt a firm yet caring request for help that evening. Her aunt called within days, saying that she would help Margaret with her medical bills and rent and would immediately send a check.

Margaret was also challenged to get out of the box the day following our session when a neighbor, whom she did not know very well, said to her that if she ever needed money, there was "some sitting in a bank that I don't need." The neighbor said that she would be happy to lend Margaret what was necessary, and Margaret agreed. Had she been in the box, she said, she would never have accepted the money.

Taking forthright action from out of the box is the way to solve problems, and it is inherent in this perspective that we will do so. We may do it within ourselves or out in the world. Either way, our focus shifts from our pain to our actions, from upset to resolution.

Positive Thinking versus Out-of-the-Box Thinking

In order to fully understand the significance of being out of the box, it is important to know the difference between it and what has commonly been called positive thinking. Positive thinking is putting a positive slant on a difficult situation instead of taking action or making concrete changes to affect it.

For example, if you were deeply in debt and worried about finding money to pay the rent, positive thinking would tell you that the universe will take care of you and you should not worry about it. In reality, you would still be in the box because you would merely be masking your fear, anxiety, and worry with what I would call a positive-thinking Band-Aid. You'd be slapping a positive thought on top of a negative situation and expecting that the mere thought would turn it around.

But when the positive-thinking Band-Aid is taken off, underneath it there is a situation that has not changed at all. No matter what you hope for, you are still deeply in debt. Positive thinking is a step, but it just isn't deep enough or pure enough.

Practically speaking, from out of the box, you would make a plan to get the money you need. You would either figure out a way to earn it, as by finding extra work, or a way to borrow the money with a clear plan for paying it back. The out-of-the-box perspective leads you to a deeper understanding or resolution rather than to a superficial explanation. That's the difference.

When we get out of the box we see things as they are, undistorted by the ego. We do not have to *try* to be positive about ourselves or our life, we naturally *are* that way. We feel better, more expansive, unstuck, and lighter, so we automatically see our life in a more positive light. We are focused on, and acting on, what we can do to create the life we want. We are in charge.

Whatever must be accomplished, that is exactly what we will do. We do not focus on how upset we feel but on how we will succeed. We face directly into the issues at hand and have the will to overcome them. We create change.

The Light at the Beginning of the Tunnel

In my psychotherapy practice, profound results often happen quickly. I think it's useful to hear the stories of others so that you can trust that the possibility of making instant and incisive changes in your own life is there as well. You now have the tools to make these changes, and I know you will. Trust that there is a light at the beginning of the tunnel, and it can shine forever in your life.

For the past two summers, I have worked as a psychotherapist at a holistic learning center in upstate New York. Here people interested in pursuing a variety of interests including personal growth, spiritual growth, women's and men's studies, health, improvisational dance, music, and many other areas come together for weekend or weeklong courses. Because they were there for such a short time, I usually met with them only once. It was therefore the perfect opportunity to teach the process of getting out of the box to help them quickly find answers to their dilemmas. Here are some examples that may be useful in understanding your own in-the-box thinking.

A middle-aged psychotherapist came in concerned that she was unable to express her feelings after her mother's recent death. She had discussed this with her regular therapist, who thought that there must be a "deep emotional problem." This was amazing to me because I saw a very competent, caring, expressive, loving woman sitting across from me. I told her I did not agree with this assessment of her at all. From in the box she was judging herself quite se-

verely. During the session, she was able to put the issues aside and ask herself, "If I were in a loving space right now, what would I be feeling about my mother? What would I feel about myself?"

When she got clear she realized that the lack of response was a reflection of her lack of closeness with her mother when her mother was alive. She was able to think of several people and things she did love. It made her realize that she wasn't unable to love, as her ego had been suggesting when she was in the box.

Then there was Kathy, who was planning to quit an unsatisfying job after many years of tolerating her unhappiness yet couldn't shake the feeling that she was "running away" from her problems and responsibilities. Despite her husband's support, she felt there must be something terribly wrong with her. She was brought up to believe that you never quit anything.

When she put the judging and invalidation of herself "on the shelf" and asked, "If I could have any job in the world, what would it be?" she realized that she would choose to follow her lifelong yearning to pursue creative work. Instead of feeling weak, Kathy saw this move as courageous. She later wrote me that she loved her new job as a creative consultant.

Robert, a thirty-three-year-old published novelist, expressed his frustration at being unable to pursue his writing career. He was plagued by self-doubt, which he felt stemmed from a critical father who never acknowledged him during his childhood or celebrated his success as an author. From in the box, he was stuck in anger, resentment, and doubt. Putting that all aside, he asked, "What if I felt passionate about my work? How would I express it? What if I stopped blaming my father for my problems? How would I feel about him? About myself? About my work?"

He realized that it was time to give up hoping for acknowledgment from his father. He felt able to begin a relationship with him from a sense of empowerment and worthiness. These realizations allowed him to begin writing again without any sense of guilt, anger, or resentment.

Finally, there was Christina, a modern dance teacher from Pennsylvania. She had planned her entire summer vacation around a particular improvisational workshop. She was looking forward to meeting and interacting with other committed, talented dancers who had similar interests. After a few days, she felt surprisingly unable to fully express herself. She became self-conscious, and the dancing ceased to be enjoyable. She saw this as a serious problem and was very upset.

During our conversation she realized that it was the emotional demands of her classmates that were weighing her down and making it hard to move or dance. At the beginning of the week she had been a compassionate listener and available to anyone who needed a companion or a shoulder to lean on. But it was becoming too demanding and sapping her energy for what she really wanted—to dance freely. By asking, "How would it feel if I were dancing as free as the wind?" the answer she received was "Take time for yourself; be good to yourself; and the dancing will follow."

A Final Word

I can think of no better way to end this chapter than with a statement made by Arthur, a client who has chosen to leave the corporate world for a life filled with deeper satisfaction. He has been using the out-of-the-box process for several years and has deeply embodied its perspective. He recently said of the process:

The real power of this process for somebody like me is that you trick yourself into knowing that it works. You're told to imagine yourself moving out of the box and experiencing the boundless freedom of being entirely unrestrained, to the point where even your physical body has no boundaries. If you're able to feel these feelings, you have made a huge discovery— that you do have power over how you feel. You have success-fully unmasked the real culprit behind your agonies, and it's not your circumstances but your mind. Change your mind (or at least disengage it), and you can feel the inherent positive power of life lift you up as if you were strapped to a thruster rocket.

4

Mind Tricks and Countermoves

You Can Teach an Old Ego New Tricks

> If the doors of perception were cleansed, everything would appear to man as it is, infinite. For man has closed himself up, till he sees all things through the narrow chinks in his cavern.
>
> —WILLIAM BLAKE, *THE MARRIAGE OF HEAVEN AND HELL*

This chapter is divided into two sections. The first section focuses on the clever tricks your ego will use to keep you thinking there is something wrong with you and to keep you from using this process. The second section describes seven ways to recapture and maintain your control. You will learn countermoves to the ego's tricks, how to build your out-of-the-box muscles, how all paths lead you home, how to write a foolproof prescription for getting free, how to let things be, how to take action rather than analyze problems, and how to have a one-pointed focus and trust your heart.

This chapter will help you to identify, laugh at, and triumph over that tricky critter the ego, using powerful tools to see through its distorted view of you and of the world.

Section One

Old Images in a New Mirror

The "I" is a concealed thief,
and it must be uprooted from the mind.
It sneaks into a person and poisons him,
and the person does not know, and does not sense this at all,
for the afflicted one does not know that he is afflicted.

—RABBI MENACHEM-MENDL OF KOTZK

The last thing the ego wants is to be ignored. It wants our attention and will do whatever it takes to get it. It speaks to us incessantly about all sorts of painful, demoralizing, worrisome, and threatening eventualities, most of which never occur. It is amazingly resourceful and quite tricky in its fight for dominance over our life. But once its tricks are identified, it is revealed as a shadowy entity that mechanically and repeatedly creates pain and illusion in order to maintain its superior position over us. Now the game becomes interesting.

The ego's voice is easily recognizable. It says things like "It's too hard," "Who cares?" "I can't," "I don't want to," and "There is something wrong with me." But once we begin to understand these tired old messages, the ego begins to lose its power to deceive, depress, and discourage. We are then able to see ourselves and our lives with new clarity.

Once you learn the language of the ego, you will not be caught in its tangled web and will ignore what it says. Your newfound wisdom is the result of seeing things more objectively—that is, as they truly are.

From in the box, you allow what occurred in the past to define who you are and how you see yourself. From out of the box, what has happened to you in the past becomes simply that—events in your history. You no longer need to forget, overcome, or resolve them, because you are no longer responding from that old self. In this way, the past does not influence or affect who you are right now.

This is not to discount the fact that you may have experienced very hurtful things in the past. But from out of the box, how you respond to your history becomes a choice. Whether to forgive or not is up to you, but you are no longer enslaved by what happened or the way you have always viewed it. You can see it with greater clarity. Please take the time to look into this matter. There may be something quite wonderful awaiting you on the other side.

Clients, especially if they have been in therapy for some time, often arrive at my door with a clear description of how they have been hurt and damaged by their parents. But when they get out of the box, they can see that whatever happened to them in the past could not have damaged their true self because it is protected, as if by armor, from the harsh effects of any emotional trauma.

An attractive, well-dressed woman named Betsy came to see me for help with her "insecurity." She was a successful businesswoman who felt she could not excel in her work because she was too concerned about being liked. This, she feared, would interfere with making tough decisions. She said that as an only child, her parents "smothered," "controlled," and "lived their life" through her.

In our first session, she saw from out of the box that her parents had done the best they could to raise her and care for her. She realized that all the love she had received not only gave her the confidence to be successful but also gave her the ability to work with people in a respectful way.

From this new perspective she saw that there was nothing wrong with what her parents did, and even if they were not perfect (and we can rest assured they were not), "nothing they did could have hurt me because I seem to have come out OK." As soon as she saw herself as emotionally healthy, her parents were instantly off the hook. When she got free, so did they.

You might not be as willing to see your parents in this new way. Your beliefs about what they did might be firmly entrenched, and we know how the ego likes to hold onto such magnificent pain. Like Betsy, when you free yourself from the anger about what they have "done to you," you will see things quite differently. If you accept that you are unscarred by them, then the anger and blame will disappear.

Alternatively, you may want to take another tack by asking yourself, "If I knew that I were fundamentally fine, how would I see the effect my parents had on me?" You might also be willing to ask yourself, "From a commitment to ending my resentment and discomfort with my parents, how would I see what they did? Am I willing to move on? How would it feel? Would I be willing to maintain this new perspective? Can I finally let them off the hook? Is there anything I would lose by doing so? Something I would gain?" Letting go of your historical suffering could turn out to be an extraordinary gift, not only for you but for your parents as well!

The ego has many subtle and not-so-subtle ways of keeping you in the box. It has one purpose in mind: to keep you committed to a negative, limited, discouraged portrayal of yourself and to thwart any attempts to see through the chinks in its armor. It must manage all information, new or old, that comes in, so that you won't be tempted to look elsewhere for counsel about yourself. Its determination imprisons you in a self-image it constructed long ago.

Below are some examples of the clever tricks and compelling arguments your ego will serve up *specifically* to keep you from getting out of the box. They usually take the form of negativity, cynicism, and self-doubt. Unless you recognize its tricks, you will be duped every time.

Remember, the ego feels it is fighting for its life, so it's pretty resourceful. The only question is, who will win this one? I submit that you have the tools to prevail.

Take a few minutes to complete the following exercise. Add your favorite tricks as you uncover them.

Tricks of the Ego to Keep You In the Box
Exercise 8

The only way to know when you are taking the ego's thoughts as your own is to recognize its voice and recognize how you feel after it speaks. Here are some of the ways it will attempt to stop you from using this process. See how depressed and pessimistic you feel after reading the list. See how successful the ego is. From out of the box, how accurate are its statements? As you look at the list and read on through this book, add your own special ways of keeping yourself in the box. Then, on a separate piece of paper, create your own list.

1. It's just too hard to get out of the box right now. It will take too much effort. I don't want to. I'm too tired. It's not worth it. I can never solve my problems with this process. I might as well just stay where I am. It's not so bad anyway. My life is so tangled that it is just too complicated to unravel the threads. Why try?

2. Given my upbringing and the difficulties I now have, this process will never help me. I am who I am. I can't really change anyway.

3. This is just positive thinking. It is too superficial to help me.

4. This box is what is real.

5. I can't do this alone. I need someone to help me or save me.

6. I should already have mastered this. I knew I would never get it. My problems are much too difficult for this process. What is wrong with me, anyway?

7.

8.

9.

10.

You can see that the ego is simply not on your side when it comes to getting out of the box. But the good news is that you don't need it, and it can't stop you when you make the choice to be free. Why? You know the answer—because being free is already yours for the asking. It is already there waiting for you. I can't repeat this enough, because the ego is terribly threatened by any glimmer of this possibility, but you don't have to be.

You can come to realize for yourself that the freedom of which I speak is yours for the taking. Jesus meant it when he said, "The kingdom of God is within you." He also tried to convey the simplicity of it by reminding followers, "Knock, and the door will be opened." He did not say it would take a lifetime. Nor did he recommend years of psychotherapy or spiritual practice. His message was to simply "seek, and ye shall find," which is not unlike the message of many spiritual teachers that the path and the goal are one. This means that if you are *truly* living your life in search of the truth, your actions will reflect what you seek. You simply need to knock and trust that the door will then be opened for you. The choice to do so rests within.

Section Two

Seven Ways to Recapture and Maintain Your Control

Now that you've seen the many faces of ego control, it's time to learn how to recapture and maintain your own control.

Learning Countermoves to the Ego

The ego's attempt to keep you securely in the box shows itself in innumerable ways in your daily life. For example, if you want to find a meaningful relationship, it will tell you that you are not good enough or that you will be rejected. If you are trying to win a tie-breaker during tennis, it will tell you that you're going to blow it. If you have a great deal of work to accomplish, it will tell you that you will never get it finished on time.

As you begin to recognize these messages for what they are, you can find ways to think and act that give you the freedom to move in more productive, useful ways. Your attention then becomes focused on achieving success rather than on avoiding failure. This makes a huge difference in the way you act.

*　　*　　*

Instant exercise—a countermove:

Think of an issue in your life that "makes you" feel stuck. Then put that issue on a shelf and get out of the box.

Once you are out, look back at the issue you are dealing with, and ask yourself, "What is the first step I can take to accomplish what I want? Is there anything stopping me from doing so? If so, how will I overcome or resolve it? When will I begin?"

These questions will show you the way and/or give you what you want. They are *countermoves* to the ego's telling you "You can't do it. It's too hard. You're not good enough. You'll fail." From out of the box, you choose to see the issue from a commitment to resolving it in the most effective way. *You ask questions that presuppose that there is nothing wrong with you or in the way of what you want.* The questions assume that there is room to move and that all you need is the correct direction.

Choosing to be out of the box rather than in it focuses you in an entirely different direction—from limitations and excuses to solutions and effective action. While the in-the-box perspective reveals few options, the out-of-the-box perspective reveals a myriad of them, plus the expectation of something new.

Here are some examples of in-the-box thinking and the out-of-the-box questions or countermoves that you can use to recognize the ego's meddling. By using them you inject rational thought and insight into any situation you confront. As always, the most important part is to identify the specific ways in which you stop yourself from moving ahead.

Countermoves for Getting Out of the Box
Exercise 9

In-the-Box Thinking	Out-of-the-Box Questions
I'll never get this finished in time.	What is the first thing I can do now?
What is wrong with me that I am not happy-satisfied-worthy-loving?	What if nothing were wrong with me? How would I see myself? How would I feel? What would I do?
I want to eat everything I see.	If I were committed to being really healthy, what would I eat?
I'll never find a good relationship.	What if I trusted that someday I will meet a person who complements my interests and satisfies my needs? How would I live until then? What would I do? What if I were complete the way I am? What will make me happy? How would I feel about my life then? What if I truly liked myself? How would I enjoy my time alone?

Now that you've read my examples, on a separate sheet of paper list ten of your most cherished, familiar, or annoying in-the-box beliefs or attitudes, and come up with an effective new question for each one that will lead you back out of the box. You will know when you are out when you feel a sense of possibility or satisfaction or if you are taking effective action to move ahead.

You can see that the "problem" is not that there is something wrong with you but that you accept it when the ego says there is. Once you recognize the in-the-box feelings the ego produces, you can immediately decide that you won't stand for it. Then you can ask yourself the questions that will lead you out of the dark and into the clear light of a beautiful, fragrant day. You will know which way to turn and will easily be able to do so. You will leave your past suffering behind and want nothing to do with it. There will be some sense that you are leaving an old friend, but I assure you that the person you become, your true self, will be much better company for you, and certainly more fun.

Granted, the ego makes very compelling arguments in favor of its perception of reality. It is quite believable. So you must be especially attuned to the sound of its voice and the feelings it evokes. If you are not watching and alert to its tricks, you will unknowingly start down a path that will leave you far from where you want to go. To be free of this human dilemma, you must respond with a certainty and strength that challenge the veracity and tenacity of the ego. You must reclaim your life, and never turn back.

Building Your Out-of-the-Box Muscles

I have found it very useful to think of gaining proficiency at getting out of the box as less of a psychological matter—because there is nothing that must be "fixed" before you do it—and more like strengthening muscles, since it takes practice, not therapy. It is much like learning to use Nautilus equipment for the first time. You don't have to be born with a propensity for using Nautilus machines, nor do you have to take a semester-long course in it or be physiologically minded. You just need someone to show you how to work the equipment. (That's my job.) To use a Nautilus successfully, you do have to be interested in what it has to offer you— building muscles. In the same way, without an abiding interest in being free from your suffering and emotional upsets, you will not use the out-of-the-box process. Therefore, practice and intention are essential.

How often and when are the best times to practice? Truly, any time is fine as long as you remember to do it. You can take two or three minutes to consider the questions "If I were out of the box right now, what would I be thinking about? What would I be experiencing? What would I be doing?" I can't make it any simpler than that—or more effective. If a regular routine of practice works better for you, then I suggest you do so at least four times a day: when you wake up, before lunch, before dinner, and at bedtime.

Additionally, use the process the moment you realize that the ego is generating negativity and doubt. What the ego tells you is no different from what everyone's ego tells them. It's nothing personal. With this in mind, it will be easier to disregard what it has to say because you know that its message simply reflects what egos do at challenging times, and not just to you. Your responsibility is to remember this truth, no matter what you are feeling at any particular moment.

It is crucial to recall that no matter how distant this perspective feels, it is still right at your feet, like a child waiting for you to pick it up. Trust this alone and you will be well on your way to mastering life. I truly mean this. Just remember that nothing is in the way of your being free except the thought that you are not. With this understanding and the unswerving intention of finding your true self, you will succeed. It is inevitable.

All Paths Lead You Home

There are many ways to get to the out-of-the-box perspective and to your own true self. The questions that you choose to ask yourself are really the keys that most effectively get you there. Just make sure you're out of the box first. Being in the box produces questions like "Why am I so stupid?" and "Who would marry such an unattractive person?" These questions will lead you absolutely nowhere except deeper into the box.

Several paths of questioning are listed below. You do not have to choose one exclusively over another; you can use several of them all mixed together. But it is useful to understand that certain paths may speak more clearly to you than others. Here are a few examples.

The path of thought or action: "If I were fully out of the box right now, what would I be thinking about? What would I be doing? How would I approach the challenge before me?"

The path of the spirit: "If I knew that my true self were right here waiting for me, how would I return to it? How would life look to me? If I accepted that what I've experienced when I was out of the box was real and true, how would I live?"

The path of the heart: "How would I feel if I were living from my heart right now? How would my body feel? What would my experience be? What would I be doing?"

The path of religion, or God: "If I were looking through the eyes of God, what would I see? How would life appear to me? How would I view myself? How would God want me to feel?"

The eclectic path: "If I were out of the box right now, what would I be experiencing? What would I be thinking about? What would my heart be saying? What would I know to be true? How would I respond?"

Use your heart, mind, and spirit. It doesn't really matter what path you take, as long as you seek the truth and surrender to it. Simply respect your true self by acknowledging that it exists and by giving it expression. You are the only one who can.

Draw Yourself a Map

As I briefly mentioned earlier, when I first learned of the possibility of shifting my awareness to this perspective, I used to sit and write about how life would look from this seemingly distant place. I wouldn't stop writing until my perspective had shifted. It's still a good way for many people to stay on track.

For many years, I have suggested to clients that when they are out of the box they write a letter to themselves that they can use as a detailed road map to lead them back to clarity. Just like the map in your glove compartment, you can take it out whenever you feel lost. It's extremely helpful. The letter reminds you of what is possible and gives you insight into how you got lost. But more important, the letter will explain exactly how to get back home to what is true and real.

I find this an extraordinarily helpful tool for people because it addresses head-on their favorite tricks to keep themselves stuck. Here's a letter much like one I wrote to myself years ago.

Dear Warren,

I know that if you are reading this letter, you are probably stuck and feeling angry, frustrated, overwhelmed, or something much like that. Well, I am really glad that you at least had the willingness to pick up this letter because I know that getting out of the box is the last thing you want to do right now or feel able to do. So congratulations for being willing to do something about it.

You probably think that you are justified in feeling what you are feeling right now and that you literally can't, and maybe won't, be able to get to a clear place this time. That's just fine. I understand. I know how bleak it seems. I also know how real it feels and how hopeless and shut down you might be right now. You really don't want to have to go through this process again. That's what you feel, but remember, it's just the old ego hooking you again. You'll quickly see how that happened once you get out of the box. For now, let's just get you there, OK? Are we together on this? Do you need a couple more minutes before you start? Do you need to go back and reread what you just read? Are you ready to leave your pain and suffering behind?

I want you to know that you will soon be on the other side of this. But you can resist a while longer if you need to. No? Then here we go.

Take a few moments to remember how things look from out of the box. Remember the sky, and the warmth of the sun, the sounds of the water, and how it feels to breathe that warm air in so deeply. Take your time. Feel that you have no boundaries, not even the boundaries of your body. Sense that you are really free inside yourself, and free to move, and run, and jump. Know that you really want to be free more than anything else.

Take the time to let this experience come over you. Then allow it to deepen inside and fill you up with a sense of peace and profound well-being. Keep your attention focused on this alone. When you are firmly out of the box, there is no issue that you can't handle. Feel the lightness and warmth of returning to yourself.

Congratulations for being courageous enough to face your demons and for taking the personal responsibility to

get yourself free of them. Thank you for turning to me for
help and for trusting me so completely. I am so proud of
what you just did.

> *I love you very much,*
> Warren

When you get out of the box, you will see that—although
you have gone from feeling bad to feeling good—absolutely
nothing in the real world has changed except your perspective. You were completely stuck and deeply entrenched in
your pain at one moment, and you felt wonderful and free
the next. All that changed was your willingness to get free of
your entanglement with your feelings. That is all, and that is
everything.

From that moment forward, you can never again make the
claim "I can't help how I feel." You'll see that this long-held
assumption is a breathtaking lie that reveals your ego as the
liar.

Take the time to revise your letter as you discover effective
new ways to convey this understanding to your stuck self.
This will become a foolproof method for getting unstuck. You
will be grateful to have this tool in your back pocket, as I often was. It reminded me of what was true, what I really
wanted, and how I could get back to myself.

You Don't Have to Kill It, Just Let It Be

The Beatles had it right. If you let the ego say what it will,
and you become uninterested and unattached to what it says,
you will find the true self that longs for liberation. You don't
have to stop the ego's endless drone but simply "let it be."

If you deeply want to be free, the voice of the ego will take
its rightful place in the background of your thought. Its voice

will probably always be there, but from out of the box you can watch it diminish in size so that it becomes insignificant to anything that matters to you. As in *The Wizard of Oz*, the demise of the powerful Wicked Witch is accomplished simply with water. The same can happen to the ego. It can literally shrivel away to a mere shadow of its former self when you apply these processes to your life.

Like the Wizard himself, one of the ego's favorite mechanisms of control is being harsh and judgmental. If it is tough on you, it scares you into inaction and emotional retreat. If you stop responding from this fear and let it be, the ego will be seen for what it is—a weak, small-minded, shallow voice from behind the curtain, which needs your interest and belief in its existence to have any power or control over you. With your consent, it's all-powerful, and it's nothing without it.

A sense of freedom and well-being revert back to you, where in reality it has always been. You are free to respond however you want, and you can no longer claim that the possibility of freedom does not exist at any time and any place. Being free becomes a choice. It is yours if you step out from beneath the crushing weight of human suffering and into the light of awareness.

Analysis or Action—You Decide

When you are stuck, you might believe the reason is that you are justifiably afraid, confused, insecure, overwhelmed, or angry and unable to do anything about it. This is just where your ego wants you: standing still and in conflict. It can rest assured that you will probably do what you have always done: let the emotions get the better of you. The ego's job is to keep things from changing.

One of the best ways to overcome the inertia created by the ego's incessant need to focus your attention on what is wrong with you is to take action. Doing so from out of the box reminds you that you are in control. Remember, action is always possible, no matter what you are feeling. The fact is, feelings can never stop you! It's your response to them that can. For example, you can get overwhelmed by a job and sit there for days in confusion. Or you can shift your perspective from one of feeling overwhelmed or stuck to one of action.

From in the box, your feelings are monumental obstacles. From out of the box, they are meaningless because your interest rests solely with responding to the immediacy of life. Because life is always in motion, what is often called for is action that keeps you changing along with it. But old images of yourself restrict you from participating. You are just not interested. You wind up feeling that life is passing you by.

When you are acting from your commitment to being out of the box, it is impossible to stay stuck. It's one way or the other. You can either continue doing what you have done in the past, by focusing on what is wrong, or you can change your perspective and start responding to what is necessary to move ahead. You can either be in your feelings or in action.

Mark came to see me for a session last summer at the holistic health center where I was working. He was there for the summer in their work-study program. He had been in therapy for many years and came in to discuss his pain about feeling separate from others. Thirty-one years of age, he had never been married or had any close relationships with women. He described how he had left a dance party after a short time the previous weekend because he was feeling so self-conscious and separate from the group.

Mark said he always looked at the negative side of things, even when he visited the most beautiful places in the world.

Rather than enjoying where he was, he would begin to think about where he was going next and would feel anxious to get there. He said, "These feelings would come over me and suck me into a kind of depression." Being miserable, he felt, was his way of hurting his parents. "I've been trying to get back at them all my life for having had five more children soon after I was born." I responded that no matter what the reason, it seemed as though it was time he stopped resenting them and trying to hurt them, especially since his father had already died.

In that session I taught him to get out of the box. At one point he began to laugh. I asked him what was funny and he said that he saw how ridiculous it was to get in the box whenever he felt good.

Mark saw in that moment that he had a choice. "The feelings that come over me happen because I have believed things were so hopeless. When I am out of the box I see that I am not a victim to any thought or feeling that enters my mind. I can choose to involve myself with them or not. It's up to me." He agreed to spend no more than fifteen minutes a day with these hopeless thoughts. He was not quite ready to leave them cold turkey, because "they feel like a comfortable old friend," but he did want to begin letting go of his misery.

Mark stopped back to see me a few weeks later and said how fantastically the summer was going. He was meeting new people, enjoying the parties, and very hopeful about a woman he had met. He joked about how negative he had been about everything and said he was spending only a short time each day with those old feelings. We were both relieved.

What is most important at difficult times is to make the choice to do something besides analyzing what went wrong.

From out of the box, your commitment is to something far different from excuses for your problems. Your excuses are exposed as having nothing to do with how you act.

It works like this: If you don't act, you have your reasons for why you didn't. If you do act in the face of your reasons, you can see that they never should have stopped you in the first place. How could they? They are only thoughts. What stops you is how you choose to respond.

My mentor Dr. Bob Shaw used to say that courage is not something that one has. It is something that is revealed *after* one acts in the face of fear or discomfort. Then it is said that the act was courageous. I am suggesting that you can't wait to feel courageous before you act. You must first get clear, and then you will have a decision to make, whether to act or not. There will then be no fear in the way, stopping you before you even get to the choice.

It can be very exciting and enlivening to act in new ways and to discover that certain old worn-out beliefs no longer hold much water. The out-of-the-box perspective allows for this kind of openness because you are not holding onto anything for dear life. You feel a sense of possibility, even though the outcome of your actions is unknown. You start to want this feeling of open-mindedness more than you want anything, including the certainty of the past.

Instant exercise:

Ask yourself, "If I were open to reexamining life from out of the box, what old beliefs about myself would I immediately toss out? What updated beliefs would I begin to incorporate into my life? Am I willing to live in uncertainty in order to discover what is true?"

A One-Pointed Focus—The Path to the Heart

You are usually in two places at the same time. You are watching yourself closely, monitoring how you are doing in relation to others and the world, and also trying to navigate through life. That annoying focus on yourself, which is self-consciousness, stops you from being fully present in life or fully available to others. You remain distracted by your concern over how you will be judged. You know how painful that is. It keeps you separate and protected—which is, after all, the ego's goal.

This is not to say that you should stop being alert for danger in your environment or from others. It is to say that you have taken this fearful, protective mechanism much too far. It has become the guiding force in many of your thoughts and stops you from being with people in a deeply meaningful way. It also makes it impossible to find a sense of ease in your life.

Because you have spent a lifetime identifying with this frightened, self-conscious side of yourself, it may seem to be a dominant part of your personality from which there is seldom much relief. But when you decide that you want to give your *full* attention to being out of the box, you instantly shift your attention to your heart and to a naturally compassionate, more loving view of yourself and life. An unexpected and wonderful outcome of this shift is that you touch a profound feeling of being at rest inside and discover the safety that comes from residing in your true self. This sense of safety is the awareness that you are invulnerable to the thoughts of your ego.

The one-pointed focus on being out of the box can also put you in contact with a deep sense of connection with the world at large. With the self-absorbed ego out of the way, you can quickly start seeing yourself as part of the world instead of being separate from it.

There is truly nothing more you need to know. You can begin to live from who you really are. *Whether you feel it or not* at any particular moment is not the point. You know what is true, and from that understanding, you know how to respond. By staying out of the box, you can do your part to end the ego-driven cycle of hurt, anger, and pain on the planet.

Instant exercise:

Take a moment to ask yourself, "If I were fully out of the box right now, what would I want to give to others? How would I contribute to the evolution of a more caring planet? What would I do to help today?"

Can you see that when you are committed to the well-being of others, the needs of the ego at this moment become insignificant? Can you sense that your concerns extend to the good of the whole? Can you feel the relief of shifting your focus away from your own needs to the needs of others? Why would you let anything intrude on this extraordinary possibility for living your life? Why would you retreat back to your limited self-concern? Can you sense the thrill of having your interest shift to something much larger than yourself? Could there be anything more satisfying than this? The implications for your life are far-reaching.

Part II

5

Bringing This Process Directly into Your Life

> Within you there is a stillness and a sanctuary to which you can retreat at any time and be yourself.
> —HERMANN HESSE, *SIDDHARTHA*

In Part II you will learn a shorter version of the four-step process as well as its practical uses for resolving personal, relationship, and health issues. Each of the next three chapters will focus on one of these areas of your life. We begin this chapter by learning the two-step process. In the second part of the chapter you will learn how to resolve eighteen troublesome issues by being out of the box.

We have been through a great deal together. You've learned to recognize when you are in the box and how to get out. You have also learned how to handle the ingenious tricks of the ego. Now you are ready for the advanced course, which not surprisingly is the simplest.

Doing the Two-Step

Instead of going through the four-step process (described in detail in Chapter 3), you can often get out of the box with the flip of a switch by using a two-step process. The primary difference between the two approaches is that in the four-step process you have to put the challenging issue on the shelf until you are out of the box and can look at it with clarity. In the two-step process you can resolve any issue you're facing without the need for shelving anything. This is because the questions you use will offer additional insight into the issue, and the process of answering the questions will simultaneously resolve the issue and get you out of the box.

Taking the First Step

As you know, the first step toward getting out of the box is to recognize that you are in it. You know that you are in it if you have any of the in-the-box feelings I described in Chapter Two (for example, being frustrated, anxious, or hopeless). Because you have always believed that these feelings accurately reflect your perception of yourself and the world outside you, you have not entertained the notion that changing your perspective is a choice you could make. Nor did you realize that this choice could have such far-reaching implications for your emotional state, your relationships, your health, and ultimately your life. The next three chapters will make this abundantly clear.

An upset is often not the result of what has actually happened to you but rather of being so identified with your emotional responses to it. Being so connected to your in-the-box perspective causes you to mistake *your* perception of reality for the *only* perception of reality.

Taking the first step means that you recall how to separate from your in-the-box feelings and thoughts. Realizing this, you can detach from your usual reactions, so that you can see what is troubling you from an entirely new view. It can feel weird—even "wrong"—to completely drop your in-the-box feelings, but it also gives you a sense of authority over your life. You are back in charge. You become fully aware that you are not trapped in any emotional state or stuck with any particular response. You see that how you respond is truly up to you.

It does take a personal maturity to accept responsibility for being in the box—to acknowledge that maybe you too are partly to blame for your negative reactions to someone else's poor behavior. It is not easy to be that responsible for ourselves. You might want to be able to blame a situation or a person. Then you can feel like a victim of what's happened, and the ego's back in charge.

The ego doesn't want you to realize that you can be free of its grasp, because if you are, it will have no power over you and will become irrelevant. In fact, the absolute thrill that accompanies the choice to take back your power and leave your pain behind is amazing! There is nothing like it when you feel stuck in an upset at one moment and free the next!

I am suggesting that whatever you are thinking or feeling, you can still choose to respond from out of the box. The choice is not dependent on your emotional state but rather on the end result you want to achieve. (Remember, anger begets anger.) From out of the box, you know the right thing to do and can act accordingly. The only question is, What will dictate your response, your ego or yourself? The choice is yours.

The All-Important Second Step

The second step in the process, after you have realized that you are in the box, is to ask yourself the question(s) that will get you out. The right ones become like flashing road signs that will lead you directly out of the box.

As we have seen, the most all-encompassing questions are "What if I were out of the box right now? How would I feel?

What would I think? What would I be paying attention to? What actions would I take?" These questions, coupled with your knowledge that another perspective is available and the intention to find it, free you from the grip and misery of the ego.

This two-step approach can also be fine-tuned to resolve specific issues in your life, when the questions are designed with that purpose in mind. In this chapter you will learn to use these questions to overcome fear, hopelessness, insecurity, and many other familiar reactions to life's challenges.

Remember, the questions you ask dictate the response you get. The correct questions also open the possibility for a new view of life and of yourself. If you were to ask yourself, "How can I become the person I want to be?" or "How do I truly want to express myself now?" you would discover a great deal about yourself.

Two Steps to Getting Out of the Box: The Short Approach
Exercise 10

Think of an issue in your life right now that is putting you in the box. In order to get out, ask yourself any of the usual questions, including "If I were out of the box right now, how would I feel? What would I do?"

Once you are out, look at the issue that was troubling you and write a very specific out-of-the-box question relating to it. Then write your responses to that question. For example:

Issue—My roommate, Sarah, yelled at me this morning because I didn't wash the dinner dishes as promised.

Question—If I were out of the box right now, how would I respond to that angry remark?

Response—From out of the box I wouldn't take on her anger. Instead I would ask her why she was so angry, and I'd be open to what she had to say. I would then apologize for breaking my promise. If Sarah still wanted to "get into" her anger, I would ask her if there was another way she could talk to me about what was upsetting her.

Doing What's Right

Even when you have gotten out of the box, you may still hear the compelling thoughts and fears of the ego. They don't stop. They just become quieter and more uninteresting because your focus is on other matters.

I am suggesting that whatever you are thinking or feeling, you can still choose to do the right thing by responding to any situation from out of the box. The choice is not dependent on your emotional state but rather on your commitment to getting out. This is very important because your priority becomes above all else to do what is right. And what's right means that you act from a place of truth, caring, compassion, clarity, honesty, and humanity. This is a larger perspective than we usually have because it involves others, their needs, and more importantly, your own commitment to staying in a clear place *no matter what*.

From out of the box, you will have the clarity and courage to make the right and sometimes difficult decisions in your life because you will not be driven by the fearful, needy, doubtful, small-minded concerns of the ego.

Shelley is a very successful thirty-eight-year-old corporate lawyer. At the office she felt confident, articulate, and competent. Yet when it came to less formal situations, she always felt she was "under a spotlight" and that any mistake she made would leave her humiliated. She wanted to run and hide whenever she attended a social function. She was overcome with fear at the thought of making small talk with strangers.

In an attempt to overcome this debilitating fear, she agreed to use the out-of-the-box process at a cocktail party. The next time I saw her, she discussed what she had done. On her way to the party, she began asking herself the following questions: "What will I do to really enjoy my conversations tonight rather than focusing on my fear of being humiliated? How can I present the competent me that I know I am at work? What if I stopped focusing on myself and became part of the group?"

From out of the box, the answers to these questions allowed Shelley to keep her attention on the conversation she was having and to stop thinking about what was wrong with her. She enjoyed herself as never before, and she experienced an entirely new feeling of being at ease. She viewed the voice in her head as a useless distraction and was no longer interested in entertaining or responding to it. By doing so, Shelley did what was right, which was to join in the camaraderie of the others and give them much warmer attention than ever before. The bonus was that in return she felt better about herself.

The ABCs of Resolving Your Favorite Emotional Issues

The two-step process will be especially helpful when you focus on specific issues. You can always use the direct method of asking yourself the most general and all-encompassing questions, which are "If I were out of the box right now, how would I feel? What would I do? What would I be paying attention to?" These questions, coupled with your knowledge that another perspective exists, can free you from the grasp of the ego. But the questions that follow contain within them a new direction for resolving the upset. They also show how the issue will appear from this new perspective. By asking yourself the right questions, the emotional issues that may have defined your self-image can disappear in a flash.

Many of people's most challenging and familiar emotional issues will be examined from both in and out of the box. I have provided examples of how clients have used the out-of-the-box process to resolve the issue. I then give you out-of-the-box questions to ask yourself and to answer. They are designed to shift your focus away from what is wrong and toward a resolution of the issue.

In some situations, there is nothing in-the-box, or inappropriate, about certain emotional responses. For example, if your child has not arrived home at an agreed-upon time, that is certainly cause for worry and concern. The problem is that we view many minor issues with the same sense of panic or dread. The ego automatically responds as if it were being threatened by forces outside its control. For example, the fear of being rejected or criticized may result in a response similar to that of facing a real threat, such as a person holding a gun to our head. When we are in the box, our reactions often get us more deeply entrenched in our upsets.

The out-of-the-box questions are the road map to freedom. Using them with the intention of overcoming any upset you are feeling will, in a matter of moments, shift your perspective to one that offers a whole new range of much more satisfying responses.

I know that these questions will help you overcome difficult issues in your life. You can use them to get yourself out of the box as well as to discover how radically different each emotional reaction would be from this new perspective. I suggest that before reading them, you get out of the box so that you access the same source of information that I did when I wrote them.

Have fun with them! Don't stop until you are successful. Decide who is going to run your life—your ego or you! Discover which questions work best for you, and change the language in any way you want. I hope that you return to the list whenever you want to resolve an issue in your life. The questions for each issue are wide-ranging so that they can be used in a variety of circumstances. They can also be used whenever you want to get to this clear perspective or gain insight into your behavior. They serve all of these functions beautifully.

The issues, arranged alphabetically, are:

Anger	*(Feeling) Hurt*
Annoyance	*Insecurity*
Anxiety	*Jealousy and Envy*
Boredom	*Loneliness*
(Being) Critical of Others	*Overeating*
(Being) Critical of Yourself	*(Feeling) Overwhelmed*
Depression	*(Being) Short-Tempered*
Discouragement or Frustration	*(Feeling) Stuck*
Fearfulness	*Unhappiness*

Anger

We start with the most challenging feeling of them all. Anger is frequently the result of not getting something we want. This may include respect, love, caring, or a raise. We might be wanting someone to keep their word or complete a job at an agreed-upon time. We may feel that our trust was violated in a relationship, that we were treated unfairly at work, or that we were denied something we deserved. We wanted or expected something to happen, and it didn't. Of course, there are many degrees of anger. It depends on who is experiencing it and the kind of "injustice" that occurred.

From in the box, we respond with a knee-jerk reaction. Something happens and we react. We often don't think of the repercussions or of alternative responses. Somehow, anything goes. Often those we care most about are the victims of our strongest response. We get hurt, so we feel justified in lashing out. We find it acceptable to act this way. This sense of justification is not limited to friends and family. We also care little for the feelings of strangers that we feel have mistreated us.

Anger is such a powerful feeling that we think we cannot change it and perhaps don't want to for fear of "short-circuiting" our mental health. Therapists have often contributed to the idea that it is better to "get it out" so that it does not remain "inside us." You may have accepted the belief that it is sitting there and that you must express it to relieve the pressure—this despite the fact that you have probably experienced times when the more you expressed the anger, the angrier you got.

The expression of anger seems to open the door to remembering even the most insignificant of upsets, which may have happened years earlier. For example, Sally says, "Yeah, but you didn't change the empty toilet paper roll during our honeymoon!" Simon responds, "I know, that's because you didn't hang up your wet clothes!" The ego does get somewhat irrational, you must admit! I don't know how it stores these things, but it finds a way.

Consider the possibility that the expression of anger might generate more anger rather than diminish it. You enter that room of anger and grab whatever is on the shelves, no matter how moldy it seems to be. Not only do you pick it up, you then feel obliged to hurl it. You say things that you do not mean and recall things long forgotten. The next time you are tempted to do this, get out of the box instead, and see what there is to say. I assure you, it will be completely different.

Words like *always, never,* and *it's your fault* are sure signs that you have entered this haunted house. Feelings of despair and hopelessness complete the picture. It's the ego at its worst. You just get on that roller coaster and let it take you for a ride.

From out of the box, your response is based on what is most appropriate to the situation. The primary focus becomes taking care of yourself, saying what you need, getting what you want, learning from what occurred, and moving on in the most effective way.

You are not in a reactive mode, because *you* are in charge, not your ego. You are therefore much more likely to have the presence of mind to ask for what you need and/or to express what it was that hurt or angered you. Most of the time there is no threat to your well-being if you are out of the box, because you are secure and not threatened by another's emotional response. You know you are fine, so you can follow your commitment to taking care of yourself beyond all else. That is your responsibility.

You can begin to distinguish between what is and what is not out of the box—if not immediately, then later on when you have calmed down. If you are in the box and want to express your anger to someone you care about, do it in a way that respects your relationship and is not abusive or unkind. What that really means is, get out of the box first. Then ask for what you need or want. You don't have to ignore or bury your anger, but handle it responsibly. *You* should respond to what happened, not your ego.

I recently led a workshop in which two sisters, Doris and Dorothy, described a recurring problem they had with a third sister, Mary. Mary had a habit of organizing family get-togethers and then leaving the house to go shopping as soon as everyone arrived. One time they waited four hours with their children and husbands for Mary to return and grew angrier with every passing minute. To make matters worse, Mary never apologized or took any responsibility for ruining their time together.

They were so angry that Mary had been inconsiderate and disrespectful to them that they were ready to disown her. They were also angry at themselves for unwittingly falling into the same trap again and again.

From out of the box, they saw that they must be more definitive with Mary. First they had to tell her how her disappearing act affected them. Then, if she continued to leave, the families would go about their activities without her. Instead of giving Mary their power and resenting her for mishandling it, they could take back control and do as they wished.

They still felt that Mary's behavior was inconsiderate (and it was), but by establishing limits, their well-being was back in their hands. Both believed that Mary's behavior was unlikely to change, because she was not open to discussing it, but that need not affect their weekend plans. They didn't have to avoid her, as long as Mary knew that her actions would not be tolerated. This freed them from much of their anger toward her. The situation was not solved, but it was a start.

Here are some out-of-the-box questions to refocus your attention on what you want and to help you to do what's best:

What is more important to me now: being right or resolving the situation?

If I were out of the box, would I feel I was a victim of someone's anger? Would it affect me in the same way? Would I choose to be vengeful?

How long do I think I need to stay angry?

What do I really need or want that I am not getting? Would I be willing to ask for it directly rather than using my anger to control or manipulate the situation?

If I chose to speak from my heart, what would I say?

What would I say to a good friend who had done the same thing to me?

If I were committed to taking care of myself right now, how would I respond?

Is the anger really getting me what I want? How can I get what I want in a way that respects and protects the relationship?

Annoyance

Like anger, annoyance often results from frustration. You can either stay frustrated and feel like a victim, or you can take action to resolve it. If you act, you will learn from what happened, get a deeper understanding of what you need, and be free to move forward while leaving the upset behind.

Sharon and Arthur got married later in life and have a wonderful relationship. She is an independent woman who works as an artist. He is a very caring man who works as a college professor. Sharon loves to cook magnificent meals, and Arthur lives to eat them.

Because Arthur grew up in a family where there was enough food to feed a small army at every dinner, he felt most comfortable at a table full of food. Sharon was happy to accommodate him.

But no matter how much food there was on the table, Arthur would not take seconds for himself without asking Sharon two or three times if she wanted more food. He justified it by saying that he did not want to take the last bite just in case she wanted it. Sharon looked at the table, saw enough food for the next two days, and did not understand why he could not eat as much as he wanted and trust that she would do the same. It was annoying Sharon that so much of their dinner conversation was about how much food she was going to eat.

Arthur said that his offering of food was a small way of giving back to her for preparing the lovely meal. He felt it was merely a reflection of his love, but agreed that he could express it in other ways, like saying "Thank you."

From out of the box, Sharon could acknowledge that Arthur's primary focus was on taking care of her. Instead of having her annoyance escalate into anger, Sharon reminded Arthur that she always took care of herself where food was concerned because it was a passion of hers.

They agreed that he could ask her once during any meal if she wanted some more food. He had to trust that if she said no, she meant it. As hard as it was for him, he had to stop asking. Getting out of the box allowed them to discuss their feelings in a loving way, and it dissipated their annoyance and potential anger.

Try using the following out-of-the-box questions when you are annoyed:

If I were being compassionate and patient, how would I respond to what happened? What would I say? What would I ask for? How would that feel?

What if I chose to use the difficulty to further our relationship? How would I express what is annoying me? What would I request?

If I were centered in my heart, how would I ask for what I needed?

Anxiety

From in the box, we make up many reasons to be worried or anxious. We tell ourselves frightening stories about what might happen to our health, our financial situation, or our relationships and then wonder why we feel scared. We can stop doing this to ourselves.

From out of the box, we would resist the temptation to distract ourselves with our fears. We would instead choose to focus on what we could best do to accomplish what we want. We know that the most effective way to accomplish what we want is to put all of our attention on it rather than dividing our attention between the ego's concerns and the task at hand.

Sophie is a fifty-one-year-old happily married woman and mother of an eight-year-old son. She called me complaining of several physical symptoms, including back and stomach pains and sleeplessness. Her physician said the symptoms were due to stress.

Sophie works as an advertising executive at a television network in New York City and is highly respected in the industry for her work and for her phenomenal success during her twenty years in the business. Unfortunately, after a recent promotion, her boss, who respected her work, left the company and was replaced by a younger, more energetic man named Joe. Joe wanted to institute many changes. Among them was to monitor Sophie's work very closely, as well as the work of those whom she supervised.

In many ways Joe was unsupportive of Sophie's work. She felt that he was trying to undermine her authority and that on a number of occasions he seemed to have set her up to fail in front of the network bosses. Because of this, Sophie was feeling extremely anxious, and in addition to the loss of sleep and her appetite she began to care much less about her work. This had never happened in her entire career. She was angry and distrustful of Joe and feared that she might be forced to quit the job.

According to others, Joe was intimidated by Sophie and her reputation for being so successful. In his first meeting with Sophie, he greeted her by saying, "I've heard you're really tough to work with." This was not a great way to start their relationship. Coincidentally, I had worked with several employees whom Sophie had referred to me, and they all said that she was a strong leader while being quite compassionate and caring. They simply loved to work with her.

From out of the box, Sophie saw that she had several options and she took them all. Rather than seeing herself as stuck and victimized by the situation, she realized that there were things she could do. She saw that she did not have to accept the treatment she and her staff were receiving, because she had the respect of the president of the division, who would often seek her counsel. He had always been an ally of hers, so she decided to tell him what was happening when he asked. She realized that Joe's assessment of her did not matter much and certainly was not worth her getting sick over. She knew that she had a great deal of support in the company and that her job was certainly not at risk.

After spending a couple of weeks thinking about what had seemed like the worst-case scenario—getting fired—she began to think of all she could do if she chose to get off the "treadmill." Thankfully, she had enough money saved so that she could even retire if she chose to do so. This would offer her more time with her rapidly growing son. She could volunteer at places she felt a kinship with, including the lo-

cal women's shelter, a maternity ward, or with young women executives. She could also take time to travel with her family, a dream she had long held.

Within weeks she felt completely at ease with whatever the outcome would be, and her symptoms soon disappeared. She did speak to the president of the division, who said he was aware of the problem with Joe and reiterated his absolute faith in her ability. He also assured her that her job was indeed secure for as long as she wanted it.

Out-of-the-box questions:

If I trusted that things would work out just fine, how would I appraise what I am worried about? What can I do to reassure myself and move on?

If I were relaxed right now, how would I see what is troubling me?

If I fully trusted my competence, how would I accomplish what I need to do?

If I were in charge of my life, how would I see what I am anxious about? Is there anything I would do differently? What would it be?

Boredom

When not fully engaged in life, human beings will be bored. Being bored is an indication that something else could be done to bring deeper satisfaction and fulfillment into our lives. From in the box, we are probably waiting for life to interest or excite us and looking outside ourselves for the source of aliveness. Our ego tells us that the situation is hopeless, depressing, or not worth the effort. As usual, the ego is mistaken.

From out of the box, we understand the way things really work: the more energy we invest in something, the more value it holds for us. We begin to invest first, then reap the rewards of that investment later. We stop waiting to receive and begin to give all we've got. Only then will the rewards be great.

If after this stage we have not gotten what we want or need from a particular situation (for example, at work), then it may be time to consider moving on. We will know that we have done everything possible to bring about change. We can then move ahead with a clear conscience, knowing that we did our best.

In the previous scenario, Sophie's anguish moved her to make changes in her life that would bring about greater satisfaction. She started working shorter hours, took Fridays off, and planned vacations. There was more to life than her work, and she decided not to wait any longer to experience it.

By answering the following out-of-the-box questions, you too will discover new ways to enhance your involvement in whatever you do:

What can I do to make my life and my work more interesting and exciting? Am I willing to make these changes? What will I do tomorrow?

How can I bring myself more fully to what I am doing?

What changes do I need to make to create more enthusiasm and excitement?

If I were feeling more passionate, how would I see what I am bored with?

If I have given all I've got and I'm still unsatisfied, what is the next step for me? What will I do to begin to make the necessary changes?

(Being) Critical of Others

You can be critical of others from both in and out of the box. From in the box, your criticism expresses judgment and resentment. You feel justified in criticizing another person because you feel that an injustice was done to you and it is

OK to "get them back." That is certainly the rationalization of the ego.

When you get out of the box, your criticism of others has the intention of making a contribution, helping, and offering useful suggestions. You are not angry, because you do not take things personally. No injustice was done to you. A person may have made a mistake, but you do not choose to be affected by it. It may be important to tell them what they have done, but you do not need to get even. You know how that would feel and what the repercussions would be. Instead, you choose the high road for the well-being of both of you. You do not have to turn the other cheek, but you are not out to destroy the other person in retaliation for what happened.

Looking back again to Sophie, she handled her criticism of Joe in an appropriate way. She first tried to accommodate the many changes he requested and to be a "good soldier," but when the situation began to affect her health, the morale of her staff, and her own emotional well-being, she decided to take appropriate action in a rational way. She discussed it with the president, Mark, and was given the assurance that changes would occur. Six weeks later Mark spoke to Joe about his attitude and the proposed changes. The changes were rescinded.

Use the following questions to guide you in making out-of-the-box criticisms of others:

If I chose to be centered in my heart, how would I see what the other person has done?

What if I were more interested in being close than in feeling superior to another? What would I say?

If I knew that we were part of a larger whole, how would I treat those around me?

Remembering that we all make mistakes, what would I say to correct what has happened?

(Being) Critical of Yourself

When you examine your actions and yourself from in the box, you are apt to judge yourself inaccurately. Depending on your propensity and the area in question, you will either judge yourself too harshly or absolve yourself of responsibility. Both come from a critical ego that either blames or can't accept the fact that your issues are exactly the same as everyone else's. You are fundamentally no different from them, despite the ego's attempt to portray you as being worse.

When you get out of the box, you see this quite clearly. You observe the human condition with all its suffering and know that you had little chance of being very different. You hadn't previously realized who you really were. Once you can accurately see who you are, what you have done, and what mistakes you have made, you can objectively evaluate the need for correction and realize that it is not helpful to judge yourself. The only need is to correct and learn from what has happened. It is straightforward and clean. There are no scars.

Recently I was speaking with a fifty-two-year-old client named Jean. She said that she knew how competent and successful she was as an actor, but at the same time she accepted the voice in her head telling her that she was not. She was deeply troubled by her doubts, despite the fact that she had been roundly acknowledged by many actors, directors, and New York critics.

From out of the box, Jean realized that she was well aware of her competence and that what she needed to do was to look from this truth rather than the one her ego was conjuring up. She saw that she had been judging herself because she had not worked in six months and was concerned about the future. She immediately began to use

*the process whenever she started to hear the faint mur-
muring of her ego speaking to her. She realized that it was
the same skill she had mastered as an actor—to fully
immerse herself in her role and by so doing ignore everything else.*

Like Jean, you are probably aware of your own competence, creativity, and confidence in many areas of your life.
Nevertheless, you continue to listen to the ego telling you
otherwise or scaring you with its concerns. You are like the
comedian who focuses solely and painfully on the one grim
face in the audience to the exclusion of the other two hun-
dred people laughing hysterically. You focus on that critical,
annoying, and compelling voice of the you-know-what.

Why do you do this? Why don't you stop? Why do you accept such limitation in your life? Why do you suffer so need-
lessly? Why am I asking you these questions that will do
nothing to get you out of the box? Because I was hoping that
you would recognize the trick and say, "Those are exactly
the kinds of questions that get me deeper into the box! He
should be asking me 'What will it be like when I act from who
I really am?' Or 'How can I be compassionate with myself?'
Or 'How can I fully express myself in the world?' Or 'How do
I really want to live my life?'"

Very good questions! Here are some more out-of-the-box
questions:

*What if I were unwilling to waste any more time analyz-
ing what's wrong with me? What if I focused instead on
what I can achieve and how I will grow?*

*What if I realized how silly it is to criticize myself? What
would I do instead? How would I live? What actions would
I take?*

What if I got really tired of the same refrain? What new song would I sing?

What if I knew there was nothing fundamentally wrong with me? How would that affect my actions?

Depression

There are several ways to make yourself feel depressed. You can tell yourself that there is no hope that things will ever change and there is nothing you can do to alter this "fact." You can tell yourself that you are less worthy than everyone else. You can also stop doing anything except sitting around and thinking about how bad—or empty—your life is. These actions would be what Bill O'Hanlan calls a good prescription for depression. If you do these things, there is a high likelihood that you will not be very happy. But you can choose another perspective.

From out of the box, you will pull yourself up and not stand for this behavior from yourself. You won't blame yourself for what you have done before, because that would be in the box, and you will know that you did the best you could do. You will discover what you can do to change *anything* in your life, knowing that the smallest step is often the most important. There is a huge difference between doing nothing, or resting in your pain, and choosing to take the smallest step forward. By now you know that it doesn't matter how you feel. What matters is that you *do something different*. You don't have to know what to do first. Just get out of the box, and the steps will appear before you.

A middle-aged therapist named Elaine was referred to me by a colleague. Elaine said that she was extremely depressed because she had to move back into her childhood home to take care of her sick mother; the man she had been dating for three years did not want a committed relationship; and she really wanted a family of her own, but time seemed to be running out. She could not sleep, was exhausted, and felt burned out with her clients. She felt hopeless and resigned that she was going to end up as an "old maid."

In the first session, I taught her to get out of the box and asked her to use the process at least ten times in the coming week. I suggested that she keep a diary of her out-of-the-box experiences.

On one occasion she got out of the box and realized that she had been completely neglecting her own needs. By asking her brother to take care of their mother for the day, she was able to go to the beauty parlor for the first time in months. She felt absolutely no guilt! That was a first.

She realized that there was room in her life for her mother and herself. By setting up a schedule and sharing the responsibility of caring for her mother, she had free time to attend church activities where she might meet the man of her dreams. As her depression lifted, the feeling of hopelessness was replaced with a sense of possibility.

Out-of-the-box questions:

If I stop telling myself that nothing will ever change, and I began to do things differently, how will I feel?

What if I stopped focusing on how I felt and began to take small steps to change my life? What first step will I take? How will I begin to get my body moving again?

What if I stopped listening to my ego's miserable ideas and decided to come up with more useful, positive, hopeful ideas of my own? What would they be? What would they say about my future? What new possibilities would I see? When will I start?

Discouragement or Frustration

Discouragement and frustration arise when you do not see another way to do what you have repeatedly done. So you keep doing the same thing over and over and hope or expect that something will change. It usually doesn't. You forget that what is necessary is an entirely different approach to what has gotten you stuck. Couples have an uncanny way of creating this dilemma.

Judith and Peter had been married for many years. Judith was frustrated at Peter's repeated ignoring of chores around the house. He did not take out the garbage when it was full and did not offer to take the laundry to the cleaners. Judith realized that for almost twenty years she had been frustrated and discouraged by his insensitivity. She needed a new plan of action for Peter to finally understand the importance of her needs.

From out of the box, she could get what she needed. She saw that there was no need to blame or hurt Peter. After all, she knew that he loved her and would do anything to make her happy. She also did not need to take Peter's actions personally. They did not reflect at all on his caring for her. They only meant that a solution was necessary. This could be accomplished with communication and negotiation.

They decided that each week Peter would go to the laundry on Monday or Tuesday. He also agreed that whenever he went to the garbage pail, he would see if it needed to be emptied. If so, he would empty it sometime that day. He would not ignore it or put it off as he had previously done. They never needed to discuss the issue again. It was resolved. Many times what is being called for is a different approach rather than an emotional reaction.

If you were out of the box, you would view the state of being discouraged or frustrated as dwelling on a problem rather than on what you can do to change the situation. You would make the choice to do what was necessary rather than contemplate your pain.

Out-of-the-box questions:

What if I were hopeful about accomplishing what I wanted? How would I go about doing it?

What if I stopped complaining and got moving in the direction I want to go? What would be the first step?

What if I saw this situation from an entirely new perspective? What options would open for me?

What if I took complete responsibility for what happened? What would be my next step?

If I were taking charge of my life right now, how would I act?

Fearfulness

So many things frighten us—speaking in front of groups, meeting new people, being intimate, being alone, changing jobs, flying, dying, the list could go on and on. From in the box, our fears often consume us and stop us from having or doing what we want. We are, as the box implies, trapped by our fears, many of which compromise our sense of being fully alive.

From out of the box, we have a very different relationship to these fears. We may still have them, but we refuse to stop ourselves because of them. We know that if we gave in to them, we would end up back in the box because we would have succumbed to the ego's need to maintain control. Fear is one of its favorite tools.

Mike came to see me to discuss the "paralyzing fears" he sometimes felt before acting auditions and at the thought of being on stage. Even though he did not feel this fear all the time, it still stopped him from actively pursuing a career in which he had been acknowledged by many as a fine actor and upcoming director. From his previous therapy, he had "learned" that his fears had their origin in his relationship with his mother. He reasoned that his self-doubts were the result of her not being there for him very much as a child.

I told him that everybody feels fear before they perform. Even Pavarotti vomits before his performances. I said, "Join the club!" The problem was not so much his fear as how he was responding to it and honoring it, even at the expense of his passion. While practicing how to get out of the box, he experienced a sense of freedom previously encountered only on the stage. He joyfully said, "I've always deeply known that this must be who I am. Now I can begin to trust it, even when I am not on stage."

For fun, I asked Mike to look at his fears from both in and out of the box, and he had a great time doing it. It was so easy for him that he realized that changing his perspective was a skill he already possessed as an actor. Of course, Mike wondered whether it would be so easy for him to make this shift before auditions, so he decided to use every opportunity to practice. Two weeks later Mike reported that he had been called for two auditions, which he said went "great." He confessed that he had still wanted to say no when he was called, but immediately got out of the box and said yes to his agent instead.

Out-of-the-box questions:
If I were committed to staying out of the box, and I felt fear, how would I respond to it? Would I let it stop me? Would I be interested in it at all, or would being out of the

box be more important to me? Would fear have any effect on my commitment to being free right now?

Am I using fear as a reason not to do what I know I should? From out of the box, what would I think of fear as an excuse not to act?

What if my favorite fear were not there? How would that feel? What would I do?

If I were out of the box, what challenges would I take on? How would I see them? Am I willing to take them on? Are they worth the risk? What would I gain?

What if I were feeling a deep sense of security within myself? What would I be able to do? What risks would I take? Would I be more vulnerable with my lover? Would I seek a new career in order to find greater satisfaction in my life? Would I be afraid of people I do not know? Would I stop worrying about my life? What other fears would disappear? What if I were not feeling that security in this moment? Would I still be willing to act from my understanding of who I am?

(Feeling) Hurt

We spend much of our lives trying to avoid being emotionally hurt. We feel vulnerable to it from many sources within ourselves and from others. For example, when we don't get what we want, we either get hurt or angry. In truth, much of our anger is based in hurt. From in the box, we can feel victimized and destroyed by what another has done to us. Hurt goes right through to our core and makes us feel the darkest depths of pain. We are almost defenseless against it. They attack, we take it on. They criticize, we wither. They're insensitive, we get hurt.

From out of the box, not only are we unwilling to be hurt by others, we are also unwilling to hurt ourselves. We recognize the invalidating, hurtful, critical conversations we have with ourselves for what they are—the ego, nothing more and nothing less. It is the human condition, and all egos do the same thing. It is nothing to take personally! With this understanding, we can immediately reject these negative thoughts as untrue and irrelevant. We can stop bowing down to these thoughts and begin to face directly into them so that we can regain authority over our lives.

This perspective also gives us the vision to see what stuff is ours and what belongs to someone else. We may not be totally immune to the damaging or hurtful effects of another, but we are able to view what they did with clarity, so that we are much less likely to misinterpret or overreact to another's words or actions. We gladly accept all appropriate contributions, even if they are criticisms of us, but refuse what can't be recycled into something useful.

This is not to say that from out of the box we would put up with abusive treatment. From this perspective, we would absolutely resolve all issues that do not support our deepest humanity. We would stand for nothing less.

Marilyn and Jane had been best friends for more than three years when Jane's house burned down. For the year following the fire, Jane rented temporary rooms. Eventually she quit her job and after months of traveling returned to town to visit friends. Marilyn insisted that Jane stay with her and offered her a small, quiet room at the back of the house. Because Marilyn and her husband were very wealthy, Jane felt that the best way to repay their kindness was to do helpful things around the house: she took responsibility for walking their dog, doing the laundry, cooking dinner, replacing the toaster oven when it broke, and so on. Everything seemed to be going along fine, and everyone got along like family.

After four months of living there, Jane asked Marilyn if she wanted to make the situation more permanent. Jane was ready to unpack her suitcases, buy some furniture, and settle down. She could either stay on with Marilyn and pay rent or move out and get a place of her own. Marilyn said she needed a couple of days to think about it.

Since Jane had not mentioned the conversation to anyone, she was surprised to find out from a mutual friend that Marilyn had no intention of letting her move in permanently. In fact, Marilyn was telling friends and her family that Jane was a "freeloader"! Jane could not believe what she was hearing. She and Marilyn talked about everything. If Marilyn wanted money or some other form of compensation from Jane, all she had to do was ask. Jane felt hurt and betrayed and was unable to continue her friendship with Marilyn until she could resolve her feelings.

From out of the box, Jane realized that she did not have to take on Marilyn's hurtful remarks about her. The remarks reflected more about Marilyn than Jane. But they did tell her that it was time for her to find her own place and that maybe it would turn out to be exactly what she needed. She was not sure if she was going to talk to Marilyn about what she had heard, but she did know that their friendship would forever be changed. From this perspective she realized that in life friendships come and go, and maybe it was better to move on. If at some point she decided to discuss with Marilyn what had happened, she would do so, but at this time she felt it better to let it go.

Had their relationship meant more to each of them, they could certainly have resolved the issue in a caring, respectful way. Almost any upset can be worked through if we listen to each other openly and respectfully. We have all seen that by resolving feelings of hurt, we are brought even closer together. But choosing to let something go that is not working in our life can also be a viable and appropriate response. From a place of clarity we can decide which direction we want to go. This is what makes the process so satisfying and rewarding.

Out-of-the-box questions:

What can I say to the person who hurt me to express my feelings without anger and without hurting them back? Is there something I need from them (understanding, compassion, respect)? What is the best way for me to get it? How can I ask for it?

If I were in touch with my strength and my sense of well-being, how would I feel about what was said and done to me? Would I still need to do or say something to resolve the situation, or can I get beyond it on my own?

From my true self, how would I respond to those old thoughts about my insecurities and my unworthiness? What will I do today to live as the person I really am? What will I do right now?

What if I refused to remain a victim to what was done to me in the past? How would I see its effect on me now? Would there be any? Would I be "scarred" by whatever occurred? What would it be like to see myself from this new place? Would I be willing to reassess my childhood and myself? Do I have the courage to see myself as completely healed?

Insecurity

Insecurity is the troubling sense that there is something wrong with us. It is part of the human condition to think this way. We either try to hide our insecurity or complain about it. Our insecurity can become an obstacle to our happiness.

The voice of insecurity sounds like this: "Everyone else is working harder but catching on more easily," "No matter what I put on I look frumpy," "I always feel so self-conscious around people." Invalidating, criticizing, and comparing ourselves with others are some of the ego's favorite mechanisms of control. We remain stuck in the painful, demoralizing feeling, deeply doubting ourselves and our abilities.

From out of the box, insecurity seems like a waste of time. We see that we can walk right through it unscathed if our intention to achieve something important is present and in our sights. If we so choose, insecurity can also be a catalyst for triumphing over challenges in our life. We can face directly into insecurity and act in the face of it. From this commitment to growth, we know where giving in leads and the pain it engenders. When we stop playing that game, we take back control of our lives.

Robbie is a forty-five-year-old massage therapist who came to see me about overcoming the insecurity she felt around people she did not know. While it had always been a problem in her social life, it had never affected her in the workplace until recently.

The problem began when the front desk started assigning her clients who were unknown to her, in addition to the regulars who requested her. She was tentative about touching the new clients and therefore gave very poor massages. Her boss knew what a great therapist she could be when she felt comfortable, but would be unable to keep her on if the insecurities continued to affect the quality of her work. It had taken Robbie three years to find an office that she enjoyed working in, so it was very important to keep this job.

After she learned the process, she said, "From out of the box, I feel so confident and secure, I don't need to compare myself to everyone else. It doesn't matter. I feel my own strength, and that's what's important."

She began to see her ego as a "wormy little thing" but also felt that she wanted to take care of it and "reteach" it about life. Robbie realized that she no longer needed to live by its rules and fears. Instead she could choose how to respond to her thoughts and feelings. She was thrilled!

Out-of-the-box questions:

What if I focus on my competence and my worth as a human being rather than on what I think is wrong with me? How will that affect what I am paying attention to? What will I do then?

What if I wanted something much more out of life? What steps would I take to achieve it? Would my insecurity stop me? Would I let it?

Jealousy and Envy

Karen, a twenty-seven-year-old single woman, came to our first session quite discouraged about not finding much work as a singer and songwriter, work she was passionate about. She said that she was terribly jealous of some of her friends who were having great success in their careers. What precipitated her calling me was an incident that had occurred during a recent performance. Trying to be magnanimous, she had invited a friend up on stage to sing with her, and to her chagrin the friend got a standing ovation. Karen had been receiving only polite applause throughout the evening. She felt envious of her friend's ability and success and embarrassed that she felt that way.

She laughed as she realized that from in the box she was carrying these "jealousy packages" regarding the success of others. She realized from out of the box that she did not need to waste time comparing herself with others but to spend more time practicing and studying with teachers that she knew could make a big difference in the quality of her performance. Rather than judging herself, she could use her passion for her work to be successful.

Jealousy and envy are insidious ways of creating pain and suffering within ourselves. By comparing ourselves with others on any number of scales—appearance, success, money, weight, cars, confidence, lovers—we torture ourselves into feeling like unworthy human beings. Because we feel so much shame about ourselves, we never talk about it to others, so we have no idea that most of us are doing the exact same thing. It is yet another way the ego controls and manipulates us into the familiar feeling of being stuck and in pain. Even worse is the insidious way in which we inflict our jealousy on others by being less than encouraging when we feel competitive with someone who seems to have what we want. Again, this is a sure sign of the ego at work.

The ego further tortures us into believing that we can never be happy without having the things that others have. It keeps us convinced that our happiness and satisfaction lie only in obtaining some object or person that we desire. If we are willing to look honestly at ourselves, we will see that getting these things can never give us what we really want, because that is not found in the acquisition of any object outside of ourselves. I invite you to look for yourself from out of the box and see what you discover.

From out of the box, we get clear about the true source of satisfaction. We know that it can never be outside of us. We know that it is always there for the taking. We know that it is who we already are. From this understanding, we would never be jealous or envious of someone else. Nor would we feel the desperation that comes from wanting what we cannot have. We've already got within us what we truly need. Everything else pales in comparison.

We might desire something and do all we could to achieve it, but we would never lose sight of the fact that we are already whole and complete exactly as we are. That's the difference.

Out-of-the-box questions:

What if I saw my true value as a human being and chose to stop comparing myself with other people? What would that be like? Can I sense the relief in doing it?

If I were complete the way I am, how would I see the habit of comparing myself with others?

What if I knew that my personal fulfillment was not about acquiring something outside myself but rather about accessing what is already waiting there within?

What if I stopped being contemptuous of what others had? How would I be with them? How would I feel about myself?

What can I begin to do to have what I want?

Loneliness

Being alone is quite different from being lonely. Being alone means simply that we are not with someone right now. It is an objective fact. Being lonely implies that there is a problem. It often means that we have interpreted being by ourselves to mean something else—that there is something wrong with us or with how we expect our life to be.

If you are feeling lonely, you need to change something in your life so that you are not judging, invalidating, or taking personally the fact that you are alone. Loneliness indicates that you may need to bring something more fulfilling into your life, such as new interests or involvements, or that you need to find a sense of fulfillment within.

Of course, you may be out of the box and still feel a sense of loneliness following the ending of a relationship. But some of your loneliness may be self-imposed and result from blaming or judging yourself for what happened rather than looking at it more rationally so that you can learn and grow from the experience. Being overly critical is not the way to treat someone you care about: yourself.

From out of the box, this treatment changes radically. You begin to do all you can to soothe your pain and take the necessary steps to move ahead in your life. You don't sit and suffer. You find the path to healing and begin the journey ahead. You are free of judgment and open to what will come.

A fifty-year-old woman named Sandy came to see me following a diagnosis of breast cancer. She was less upset about the cancer than she was about a ten-year relationship that had just ended. Finding herself alone for the first time in many years, she began speaking hysterically of her life being over. She said that she was hardly eating or sleeping and that she wanted to die. She also felt that she should be put in a psychiatric hospital to get away from it all.

She had repeatedly tried to contact her former lover, who refused to see her or reconsider his decision to break up. She felt he was being extremely unkind to her, especially in light of her being so sick from chemotherapy.

Thankfully, she was able to see from out of the box how crazy it was to threaten her health because of a man who treated her so insensitively. She saw that if this man were treating her sister this way, she would think he was being heartless. She grew to accept being alone for the time being and saw that her priority had to be recovering from the illness. This, she knew, was the only rational and healthy choice she could make, and she made it.

Out-of-the-box questions:

What if I were not blaming myself for being alone? What if being alone said nothing about me? How would I see not being with someone right now?

If there were something to learn about myself and to change, what would it be? How will I begin to make these changes in my life?

How can I begin to focus on what I most like about myself? What would it be?

What if I stopped judging myself and my life? What would I see?

If it were really great to be alone, what would I do?

What if I discovered new things I enjoyed doing? What would they be?

What is a better way to spend my time: thinking about what is wrong with me or discovering what I want? What will I do to bring this about?

If I could do anything today, what would I do? How would I most love to spend my time?

What if being alone allowed me to indulge myself? How would I do it? Would I sleep later? Take a vacation I'd always wanted? Treat myself to lunch at an outdoor café? What would be my special out-of-the-box way of indulging?

Overeating

We all come up with many reasons to overeat. Some of the reasons are emotional, and some are physical. For some, overeating is just a bad habit. I will discuss each of these factors in Chapter Seven. For now I want to say only that you can come to understand what is behind your eating so that you can make appropriate choices that support your emotional and physical well-being.

From in the box, what we eat is often based on irrational

choices. We tell ourselves things like "I just feel like it," "It doesn't really matter," "Just this once. I'll start eating healthier tomorrow," "I've had a bad day," "I've had a good day," "I deserve it," "It's fat-free." We do what we want based solely on emotions. We want it. We justify it. We eat it. There is little room for reason.

How would you choose your food from out of the box? Your choices would probably be based on some health and nutritional factors. There is certainly plenty of good information out there. Your choices might also be based on the pleasures of good food (eaten in appropriate quantities and in moderation). The difference is that you would no longer be eating unconsciously and without regard for the needs of your body.

Out-of-the-box questions:

If I were committed to my health and to truly nurturing my body, what would I eat? When would I eat it?

If I fully accepted my body the way it is, what would I eat? How would that feel? How would I exercise?

What do I need to learn about nutrition? How will I learn it? When will I begin?

What if my eating were based on rational and nutritional choices rather than on emotional ones? What changes would I make in my eating habits? What foods would I eat? What foods would I eat less of?

What if I were less concerned about losing weight and more interested in my emotional, spiritual, and physical health? How would this affect the way I think about my body? How would this affect what I eat?

(Feeling) Overwhelmed

We touched on this subject earlier in the book. From in the box, we focus on the enormous task in front of us and feel unable to complete it. We don't believe we have the resources, time, support, money, intelligence, or background information that is necessary. We see ourselves as just not up to the task. At times this may be an adequate appraisal of the situation—if, for example, we are asked to take on yet another project when we are already weeks behind on the rest.

From out of the box, we simply assess what we need to do and make a plan for accomplishing it, one step at a time. If we know that we are unable to complete it, then if at all possible we don't take it on. We don't think about what is lacking in us or why it should be some other way. If something will help us to meet the challenge, we find it. In the end, we can either do the job, or we can't. What a relief from all the turmoil and self-judgment we put ourselves through!

Another way we might feel overwhelmed is with guilt, shame, and embarrassment about something we may or may not have done in the past. These feelings can be paralyzing if we do not see them for what they are. Of course, it's the ego that keeps reminding us of these unpleasant thoughts and feelings. Nonetheless, we have to look at what we are doing to ourselves from a perspective that allows us to see the truth of what has occurred. If we have done something terrible, then we need to face it and accept it. Then we need to move on. If upon examination we find that we can finally absolve ourselves of our overwhelming sense of guilt, shame, or embarrasment, then that is our work as well. This is what Rita did.

Rita is a very bright fifty-nine-year-old mortgage banker whose second marriage is a supportive and loving one. She came to see me to discuss her pain about her thirty-seven-year-old daughter, Sara, with whom she has had a difficult relationship almost since the child's birth. Sara has lived with Rita's first husband, Martin, in Venezuela since the age of ten. Martin used to beat Rita when they were married and until this day calls her a "whore." Since childhood Sara has been very close to her father and distant from Rita.

Rita has been unable, even with the help of many other therapists, to give up her overwhelming guilt about leaving Sara at such a young age and "failing her as a mother" following her divorce. She described her usual visits with Sara as going from very warm during the first week to increasingly abusive and distant as Rita's departure approached. During their last visit, more than three years ago, a disagreement occurred in which Sara told Rita, "You are dead to me as a mother!"

Rita told me that she often found herself thinking about the day she told Sara that she was moving out and not taking her along. Sara did not say a word and just walked out the door and stood in the backyard. The last image Rita remembers is how innocent and frail Sara looked and how alone. Rita felt terrible about leaving Sara with Martin.

By learning to move out of the box, Rita quickly saw that this painful image of Sara standing in the backyard was certainly not the most useful one to focus on thirty years later, unless she wanted to torture herself. In fact, there were many reasons why Rita left Sara with her father, not the least of which was that this was what Sara wanted.

When Rita experienced being out of the box, she felt "a freedom to accept myself." She saw that the choices she had made about Sara were absolutely the correct ones. She could either choose to invalidate and judge herself for what she had done or, from a more compassionate and accurate perspective, accept and even acknowledge the appropriateness of the decision she had made at that time.

She felt that this new understanding was crucial for her well-being. She also saw that when she stopped regarding

Sara as damaged, and feeling guilty about it, she was less likely to let Sara be abusive to her, which opened the possibility that when this behavior was not condoned by Rita, Sara would stop acting like a "wounded child." This is what happened. On subsequent visits, Sara usually stopped her criticism of Rita within a day because Rita told her that she was no longer willing to be treated that way. Their relationship is far from perfect, but Rita is no longer overwhelmed with guilt and shame about what she did.

Out-of-the-box questions—being overwhelmed by tasks in my life:

What's the first step I can now take to complete what I need to do?

What is my plan for completing the rest? What tasks can I let go of? When shall I begin? When will it be done?

Can I divide some of the tasks into small ten- or fifteen-minute segments so that I can complete them in the next week or two?

Out-of-the-box questions—overwhelming feelings of embarrassment, shame, or guilt:

From out of the box, how do I see what I did? Was it appropriate at the time or not?

If it wasn't, is there something I can do to correct it or make amends to the other person? If I can't, can I choose to leave it alone?

If what I did was appropriate, am I willing to stop creating the pain I have been inflicting on myself? Will I? When?

(Being) Short-Tempered

We often prefer to feel justified in our outbursts rather than find another way to express what we don't like or don't want. Unfortunately, being short-tempered is often like sneezing or coughing without covering your mouth. It lets unhealthy energy out of you and onto anyone in your path. We also feel justified in taking our frustration or impatience out on others even though we are the ones who are tense.

How would you see this response if you were out of the box? I think it would be clear that your frustration is your responsibility, and others do not deserve to be the receptacle for your garbage. Why would you ever treat another person that way? From this new perspective, you would be able to get a grip on yourself, calm yourself down, and ask for what you need or walk away. You would realize that things may not always happen in just the way you want and that there is no reason for making someone else pay the price for your short fuse.

Alan was constantly having problems with his temper. An architect, he would often be a terror at work with both employees and business associates. He was disrespectful, mean-spirited, and highly critical of what others did and the mistakes they made.

He lost a great deal of work because of it. His bad temper extended to his home life as well. His seven-year-old son was having temper tantrums on a regular basis, and his wife of sixteen years said she felt humiliated by him and ashamed to be with him in public.

Alan had been banned from two restaurants because of problems he had with employees there. Police were even called on one occasion. He would also get enraged at having to wait in line at a local grocery store and was a terror on the road.

He always felt justified in his outbursts and had excuses for his behavior: it was not his problem but a reaction to what others were doing to him. He knew that he needed to change to prevent further repercussions in his personal and business relationships. The threat of being fired and the fear of his wife leaving him precipitated his call for therapy.

From out of the box, Alan saw that he had a choice of how to respond to his frustration. It was very challenging for him, especially at times when he was very tense, as when he was stuck in traffic or when associates were late with their work, but over time he realized that it was no longer acceptable to be so easily or willingly triggered by what he did not like.

Amazingly, his short temper was brought under control by the choice he made to be more accepting of and caring toward others rather than to focus only on his own feelings. Each week he proudly described instances in which he responded to situations very differently from ever before. He worked extremely hard, and it paid off.

He was able to return to the restaurants from which he had been banned, began to be more courteous to his employees, and was much calmer when waiting in lines and when driving. His wife was able to attest to the remarkable changes he had made. There was more work he needed to do, but he was well on his way.

Out-of-the-box questions:
If I were being compassionate, how would I respond?
If I were being patient and accepting, what would I say?
If I were fully responsible for my anger, how would I express it? What other way could I choose to say what I want?
If I were unwilling to hurt people any longer, what would I do differently?

(Feeling) Stuck

Feeling stuck can involve two very different situations. First, you may feel stuck with a difficult dilemma, unable to decide what to do. Should I leave or should I stay? Second, you may be stuck in your ability to find your way through a challenging problem. This might be a creative challenge, an intellectual challenge, or a personal challenge in your life.

In each case, what is necessary is the clearest perception you can muster to sort it through, but we often automatically resort to an emotional response because it is the most familiar. So while we say we seek security and emotional stability, the first thing we do is to sacrifice the very things needed to achieve them—rational thought and an openness to new ideas. What is necessary is clarity, free from the distortion and drama of the ego. From out of the box, we have this clarity. It is already a part of this perspective. We don't have to search for it, we only have to use it.

Abe is an accountant who lives in New York City and has been married to Louise for twenty-five years. They have three children living at home. Louise complained that for as long as she had known Abe, he had always gotten depressed and irritable on Sundays. It had been terrible for the family because they all had to deal with his bad moods, which often ruined their weekends together. Abe said that, like his father, he would get tense on Sundays thinking about all the pressures of the coming work week.

The out-of-the-box questions he asked himself were "What if I saw Sundays as an important day for the family to be together? What if I wanted to end the weekend with everyone feeling so great that it would carry on into the next week?" Once out of the box, he immediately recognized that his family deserved no less from him.

When we spoke several weeks later, he said that the process had helped him to completely overhaul his attitude about Sundays. By choosing to triumph over this old pattern, he was no longer stuck in an attitude that had controlled his behavior for decades. It's been almost three years since he experienced any "gloomy Sundays."

Out-of-the-box questions:
What if I were committed to getting unstuck? What first steps would I take?
What if I stopped complaining or being upset about the challenges I face and began to think more creatively? How would I see the challenges?
What can I do that is totally different from what I have ever done before?
If I were emotionally free from the idea of being stuck, what would I do? What choices would I make?

Unhappiness

There are times when, as decent human beings, we feel badly about what has happened to us or someone else. We may not be depressed about it, but we feel that what occurred is not what we wanted. We want happy endings. We want what we want when we want it. The ego is very good at jumping on those times of disappointment and rubbing our noses in them. It tells us they are our fault, and a variety of other unflattering things. The ego also tells us that things will remain this way for a long time and that we are powerless to change them.

You can recognize that feeling unhappy is no more than the voice of your complaints and negativity. It is the easiest, most common inner conversation to have with yourself and also the most physically and emotionally damaging. It depletes your spirit, your energy, and probably your immune system as well. You should begin to recognize the voice and immediately stop it when you do. Don't be too shocked by its frequency, and don't get into the box about it. It is, after all, the human condition.

From out of the box, you will not be thrown by the annoyances and disappointments of life. You will be in touch with a profound sense of satisfaction at simply being yourself, and you will focus on what you have rather than on what you want. There is nothing that you need in order to feel content. Your well-being is firmly in hand. You have the skills to recognize what is happening inside your head, and you can refuse to make it real by taking part in it.

Can you imagine what it would be like to be free of these automatic and painful responses to life? There would be so much less suffering. You would be so much more at ease and much happier. You would move right through upsetting issues like a hot knife through butter.

Barbara was planning a special evening for Bruce. They had been married for five years, and she decided to surprise him with an intimate dinner when he arrived home from work on his birthday. She told him that she was going to take him out for dinner but actually planned to cook a special meal of his favorite foods and have a romantic evening at home. They agreed to meet there at 6:00 P.M.

Unfortunately, Bruce's coworkers had also planned an after-work surprise, at the local bar. Bruce left the office with a couple of the guys at 5:00 P.M., and ten other buddies arrived soon after. Bruce was very touched by what they did, and they had a great time together. At 5:45 P.M. he called Barbara to say he was leaving in about an hour and that he would be home by 7:15.

Barbara couldn't speak she was so upset. She had ninety

minutes to get over her disappointment and anger at him for not keeping his word and spoiling her plans on this special night. By 7:15 the food would be pretty dry and was no longer going to taste good. She was very frustrated.

Barbara knew that her upset put her deeply in the box, and she decided that the only way to salvage the evening was to get over it. She asked herself the out-of-the-box questions "How would I feel if I were in touch with my love for Bruce and my commitment to having this be a special evening for the two of us? How would I respond to what happened tonight?"

By asking these questions, Barbara was able to fully shift her perspective. The experience of peacefulness and freedom came over her like a wave. The contrast between the unhappiness and resentment she had been feeling and the sense of well-being and lightness she now felt was remarkable and unmistakable. By turning her attention entirely to embodying this perspective, she was amply rewarded. She was free.

From her place of clarity, she easily felt her love for Bruce, her reasons for wanting to give him such a special evening, and her deep gratitude and satisfaction about all they had together. She knew how important his male friends were to him and how wonderful their gesture was. She also knew that he was usually quite considerate and thoughtful, that he had no way of knowing about her secret plans, and that this incident was an exception due to exceptional circumstances. By the time he arrived home, she was completely in love with him, and he didn't even know all she had done to overcome her pain. They were free to celebrate his birthday and their lives, which they did.

We know the effect that Barbara's unhappiness could have had on the evening. We've all thrown our best intentions out the window, despite wanting to do otherwise, when our emotions got the best of us. It is at these times that we now have a way to make a profoundly different choice. This does not mean that you "swallow" your "true feelings" of hurt, anger, or unhappiness. You should certainly discuss things together, as Barbara did with Bruce the next day. But she did so from a place that fostered closeness rather than more separation. See which works better in your life.

Out-of-the-box questions:

What if I could see the "bad" things that happen to me as learning experiences or chances to grow? How would that feel? How would my life look to me then?

What if I decided to limit the amount of time I chose to be unhappy to fifteen minutes twice a day? Could I live without it? Would I be willing to? How would I fill my time?

What if I saw my negativity as unhappiness? Would I be willing to notice all my conversations that smacked of this attitude? Would I be willing to limit them to less than 25 percent of my speaking? What else would I begin to speak about? (You might start with the weather and your hopes, dreams, and plans for the future.)

Conclusion

Here are the main points you need to remember:

1. Recognize when you are in the box.

2. Ask and then answer whatever questions work to get you out of the box.

This is the two-step process in action. Write these sentences on a piece of paper, put it in your purse or wallet, and have a great life. It's that simple.

The two-step process is an easy way to get yourself out of the box. There are two types of questions that will do the trick. In order to formulate both types, I imagined myself already out of the box. I did this by asking myself, "If I were out of the box right now, what would I be thinking? What would I be feeling? What would I be doing?" Not surprisingly, these have become the most general and often used questions in the process. It is the answer to any or all of these questions that will set you free.

The other type of question you can ask and answer is the specific issue-related kind I've written throughout this chapter. These questions will show you exactly which erroneous thoughts and beliefs have been keeping you stuck in the box. For example, if you were being short-tempered and wanted to control it, you might ask yourself any of the following questions: "What if I stopped blaming others for making me mad? What if I were more patient and understanding? What if I cared more about the way I treated others? What if I took responsibility for my anger?" These questions expose the true nature of short-temperedness and show you exactly how to change it: take responsibility for the way you are acting; be more concerned with your effect on others; be patient and compassionate; and decide how best to deal with your anger. From out of the box, you will be able to make these changes.

To change your emotional state at more challenging times, I recommend using the four-step process described in Chapter Three. The additional steps are there to remind you that when your feelings seem to have a choke-hold on you, you can simply put them on a shelf until you are out of the box and able to face them with clarity and perspective.

Another difference between the two processes is that in the four-step version, I have not given you the specific questions to use for your investigation into the source of the issue, so you are on your own. But once you are out of the box, you've got the wisdom and the clarity to solve the problem by yourself. Remember, the ego will never suggest that you look into what's getting you stuck. You know where it wants to keep you. So you make the choice.

You have two tools to select from. Both work just fine. It is up to you to decide which one you want. Do you need a hammer or a screwdriver? Only you know what is necessary. In either case, it is important to practice using both processes so that you can get out of the box in any situation you face. Some people prefer one over the other. See which works best for you. Each will help you resolve issues. Each will equip you to access the true source of clarity and fulfillment that is *always* awaiting you within.

When you access this clarity, you will know, as I do, that the primary reason to use this process is to *change*. The change will be in how you see yourself and how you act toward others. The out-of-the-box process is not just for feeling better, although that is a wonderful result. It is for changing who you are in a fundamental way and knowing deep within that change is ever possible. Remember, being free is always a choice.

6

Healing Your Relationships

> Instead of recognizing our intimate connection with all others, we create individualized forts of egocentricity, which require our constant attention for maintenance and defense. This consolidation and defense of the ego leads to a sense of isolation and imbalance—to a loss of humanity—and thus to a further limiting of our understanding of each other.
> —TARTHANG TULKU, *TIME, SPACE AND KNOWLEDGE*

Relationships can be the source of our greatest pleasure in life and also the source of our deepest pain. In the previous chapters we have focused primarily on resolving emotional issues within yourself. In this chapter, we will focus specifically on the implications of in-the-box and out-of-the-box thinking on your relationships with others. I'll help you work through some of the most challenging issues that come up with your family, friends, and colleagues and in intimate situations.

The vast majority of interactions in our relationships revolve around communication in the following five areas: asking for what you need, overcoming anger and resentment, resolving deeper hurts, expressing love and caring, deepening your intimacy and enhancing your sexuality. If we can master these forms of communication from out of the box, we are assured of attaining satisfaction in relating to others.

By focusing on each of these areas in this chapter, you will see the many ways in which the out-of-the-box perspective can help you resolve any problem that arises. We will also go beyond problem-solving to find the true source of intimacy and love.

Believe It or Not, You Might Just Be In the Box

As before, I'm including a list of in-the-box communications to get you started on this exploration and to remind you that some feelings that you believe you are justified in having might just be in the box. It might seem difficult at first to face your responsibility, but I know you would want nothing less for yourself.

Remember, all of the out-of-the-box suggestions I make in this chapter and throughout the book reflect how things appear from this perspective. I am not saying how you *should* feel or react. I am simply describing how this universal perspective changes everything.

I strongly suggest that you take a moment to get out of the box before you read the list so that you can see why the responses are so clearly in the box. Add more as you recognize them.

In-the-Box Communication

Anger
Attack
Blame
Denying your mistakes
Hurtful criticism
Insensitivity
Judgment of others
Passivity

What effect would any of these responses have on someone else? Do you think they would promote out-of-the-box responses back to you?

Instant exercise:

Now that you have identified these in-the-box expressions, ask yourself, "If I were out of the box, and I were strongly criticized for something I had done, what would I say to the person who criticized me? How would I say it? What would I need? Would I need to say anything? Could I come to terms with it on my own? How would that feel? What would I learn?"

From out of the box, might you just say that you felt hurt or angry about what you feel they did? Might you ask for an apology? Would there be any need to blame, yell, or resent them? You could even offer a suggestion for how better to approach you in the future. I think you can see that your response would come from a deeper level of caring and would be less likely to be an emotional reaction from the ego.

Often your anger (as well as most other feelings) reflects your own state of mind rather than what another has done to you. This may be difficult to acknowledge but is often true. Experiment for yourself by looking at your usual reactions and asking yourself, "How differently would I respond if I were out of the box?" "How would I respond if I were having a great day?" "How would I respond if I were deeply committed to maintaining my sense of well-being, no matter what? Would I let anything take me away from that?" You'll see the truth if you are courageous enough to accept responsibility for your part.

You walk into work on a Monday, preoccupied with planning your week. Just as you're taking off your coat, your

*boss stops you and says, "I thought I asked you to have that
report on my desk by 5:00 P.M. last Friday? Where is it?"
You storm away feeling angry and mistreated.*

Because the ego is so fragile and quick to react, it is easy to
see why we often respond to almost any provocation from in
the box. We have all done it. In-the-box responses reflect
your strong belief that your reactions are justified simply because you have them. You also think that you have few options other than to react, even when you *know* how
overblown or inappropriate the response might be. Someone
says or does something to you, and you get triggered, so you
"let it out." You tell yourself that the response is justified, so
you express it. You bow down to your feelings as if you were
their slave.

Instant exercise:
   What if you didn't respond to your in-the-box feelings as if
they ruled your life? What if you didn't bow down to whatever they told you to do? What if *you* were really in charge of
how you responded to life? How freeing would this be? Are
you willing to try new ways of responding? Could you be that
courageous? How would this affect your interactions with
others? How would life be different then?

When you cater to your feelings, you are clearly in the box.
Here are some more typical in-the-box responses. Add your
own favorites as you think of them.

You might feel:

Angry	Devastated
Critical	Hopeless
Depressed	Judgmental
Powerless	Vengeful
Resentful	Victimized

At a psychotherapy conference in California, I met a psychologist named Ilene. We began to discuss our different orientations to therapy. She is psychoanalytically trained and works with clients over long periods of time to help them gain insight into their behavior by examining all aspects of their childhood. I discussed my solution-oriented approach and told her about the process of getting out of the box. Although she was skeptical, she agreed to try it right then, to resolve a long-standing issue.

She told me that she had been in therapy for many years to resolve her feelings about the ending of her marriage twelve years earlier. She was still suffering deeply and was intensely angry at her husband for leaving her and their two small children for another woman. The woman happened to be her best friend.

I taught her to get out of the box in the same way I have described—first by imagining being in the box and then being outside of it. As she described being out of the box, she said that she would feel the way she did when she was dancing, which she loved doing. Whenever she danced she felt free, happy, light, and unconcerned about others' opinions of her. Dancing allowed her the freedom to fully express herself in a way that was thoroughly satisfying and joyful for her.

I asked Ilene to look at her life and specifically at her pain and rage from a commitment to staying with this joy. She saw how from this perspective her suffering was completely unimportant and a waste of time. Yet she also said that choosing to let it go would feel like a great loss. She had spent so many years immersed in these feelings that she experienced them as "an old friend."

She tearfully spoke of the freedom she felt at the possibility of giving it up forever. She was shocked at her ability to even consider the notion of letting her pain and anger go, and even more surprised as she felt it lift off her shoulders "like an enormous weight."

I pointed out that this new understanding did not mean that she would never think in the old way again, especially if she was not watchful. The difference was that she now knew, forevermore, that it was a choice, not an obligation. From out of the box, she knew exactly what to do if she got stuck again. She would switch to this perspective and remember what she had realized while discussing it with me. She agreed to write about what she now realized so that she could refer to it and add to it if necessary. We agreed that if she needed to, she could think about her misery but would limit the time she thought about it to fifteen minutes a day. (I learned this technique from Bill O'Hanlon many years ago.)

Ilene said she realized from our discussion that she had spent much time "supporting" clients in their pain but very little time helping them to move on. She was also touched, she said, at the tenacity with which I worked with her. I did not compromise my commitment to helping her see the light and was unwavering in my belief that this perspective was there waiting for her, no matter what, even though she felt so entrenched in her position and stuck in her rage.

Later she wrote to me saying that she was not only end-ing her therapy but had also chosen to end her pain and to move ahead in her life. She noted that her children had commented on how happy she had been. She planned to start dating as soon as possible. "My period of mourning is over. I think I've had enough. I'm beginning to live again."

Out-of-the-Box Ways of Communicating

Communicating from out of the box bears little resem-blance to communicating from inside. One major difference is that our attention shifts from being primarily on ourselves and what we want and need to being on the other person. This happens because when we are out of the box, we want and need nothing from another or for ourselves to make us feel whole and complete. We are already complete as we are. We are not looking for validation. We know who we are. It is a great relief.

This does not mean that we do not want closeness, inti-macy, communication, time for ourselves, fun, respect, or many other elements of relationship. The difference is that we are not experiencing a sense of being empty inside and needing another person to fill us up.

We can then meet each other without wanting so much for ourselves and no longer demanding or expecting so much from those we care about. We are free instead to give fully to other people. This creates a profound sense of relatedness. From this experience of relatedness, the ego no longer stands between us, because we have already moved beyond its grasp. From here there's a much greater possibility that others will meet us in a similar way. Either way, our well-being is not dependent on it.

From out of the box, our well-being is truly unshakable. It becomes much easier to listen to others more openly, apologize when we have done something wrong, and ask for what we need without fearing that we are giving everything and getting nothing in return. Our well-being is already intact, and these things will not threaten our emotional state. It takes practice to be able to communicate effectively from out of the box, especially at challenging times, but the satisfaction we'll receive is worth every ounce of effort.

In the remainder of the chapter we'll learn to deepen and broaden your out-of-the-box ways of communicating. Specifically, we will learn to:

> *Make requests rather than demands*
> *Move from criticism to compassion*
> *Express what we feel without anger or blame*
> *Overcome our resentments*
> *Be clear as opposed to being nice*
> *Resolve deeper hurts*
> *Deepen intimacy and sexuality*

Making Requests from Out of the Box

Asking for what we need is easier for some people than for others. From in the box, requests usually have some kind of irritating aspect to them. They might be demanding, needy, angry, or hopeless. It is difficult to give to someone who is coming from any of these positions. It's just not satisfying, if not altogether unpleasant, to give to them when they are expressing these feelings along with their request. This is because the ego focuses on the negative, needy, angry side of the desire.

For instance, you know how annoying it is when someone you care about asks in a demanding way that you buy something for them. It takes a great deal of compassion to get past wanting to say no, even if you wanted to give it to them in the first place. When you make the choice to respond from out of the box, your attention shifts back to your heart, your compassion, and your desire to give.

Sharon had come to dread her birthday and Christmas. It wasn't the passage of time that upset her but her disappointment with her husband's gifts. While Ian always bought her something lovely, she was inevitably saddened that he didn't seem to know her well enough to choose something that she truly wanted. She came to a session with me upset with the expensive gold necklace he had bought for her birthday. She knew he had made a great effort to buy something she would like, but she really wanted pearls.

After she was introduced to the out-of-the-box perspective, she was able to see that there was a very simple solution. Because she knows that Ian loves and cares for her, she knows he would probably also love to know what she wanted as a present. She realized that she had not discussed her desire for pearls and that his choice was tasteful and elegant.

She then felt she could thank him for what he had given her and, if a future moment seemed right, could discuss how her heart had been set on pearls. She was committed to taking care of him in the process, as well as getting what she desired, and thought they could have a wonderful time together picking out the gift.

From out of the box, Ian felt acknowledged for what he had done and did not take her desire for pearls personally. He was happy to get her what she preferred, which was, after all, what he wanted to do anyway. They did have a wonderful day together and were grateful to have a useful way to deal with this potential upset. Their ability to handle this with respect and understanding brought them even closer together.

From out of the box, asking for what you need is like a breath of fresh air. It is a simple, direct request that is pure of heart and with clear intention. If you, as the listener, are also out of the box, you almost always want to accommodate a request that comes from this place. What else could be more satisfying than to give to another who is also giving of themselves?

Instant exercise—out-of-the-box requests:

Think of something you want emotionally from someone you care about. Then consider how you would ask for it from out of the box. How different would your words and your tone be from this perspective? The difference should surprise you.

From out of the box you might also ask one of the following questions:

If I trusted that I would get what I want, how would I ask for it?

If I asked for it from my heart, how would I phrase the request? How would my tone of voice sound?

If I were not angry, what would I say?

If I felt deserving of it, how would I ask for it?

How different would your request sound from this perspective? Why not make the request from this perspective and see what response you get?

From Criticism to Compassion: How Couples Use Out-of-the-Box Thinking to Create a More Loving Environment

One of the most rewarding aspects for me in using this process is watching couples make profound changes in their relationships. I've learned that when we choose to look from this new perspective, our anger, frustration, resentment, and hurt fall away. Although earlier we may have been interacting from the desire to win fights or get our way, now we start choosing to interact from a commitment to each other and to deepening our relationship. We discover what we hoped our relationship could be: a respectful, open, accepting, fun, and loving way of being together. Our relationships become much easier because respect for each other—and our differences— becomes the context through which all else is seen.

This is a natural response when we are out of the box because inherent in this perspective is a concern for the other. There are two reasons for this. First, we experience that there is nothing wrong in ourselves, so our concern can broaden to include the well-being of the other. Second, anger and resentment literally disappear when we choose to foster a deeper connection rather than focus on just our own personal needs. We become less concerned with protecting those needs to the exclusion of the other and realize our shared commitment to something more important.

It is a beautiful and magical moment when couples drop their fear and anger and experience their sense of connection. It's a choice they learn to make not only at easy times but especially at more challenging times.

Many couples who have sought help have repeatedly acted in the same knocking-your-head-against-the-wall way. They expected, but never got, a different result. They quickly discovered, from out of the box, that they could use a whole new range of options to resolve even the most long-standing and painful difficulties. They began to focus on finding solutions rather than on rehashing old problems.

They stop fighting about taking out the garbage and come up with a plan. They stop complaining about not spending enough time together and make a date. They stop criticizing each other's insensitivity and ask for what they need. They stop making demands and start speaking from their hearts.

Larry and Mimi are in their early forties and have been together for six years. She is a successful lawyer, working hard to make partner in her firm. He is a writer who is involved in spiritual study. He had become extremely frustrated by their lack of time together and their low level of intimacy. He told me during our initial telephone conversation that he was doubtful that their relationship would survive, and he was angry and disappointed. The couple's therapist, who had been working with them for many months, recommended that they see me before making a final decision, and they agreed.

They came to the first session highly skeptical that anything could bring their relationship back together. They were each very angry and blaming the other. Larry felt that Mimi treated him with little respect, and Mimi felt that Larry was condescending and critical of her. They were both prone to angry, long-lasting fights.

In the second session, I taught them to get out of the box. Larry realized that the out-of-the-box perspective was much like what he had experienced at other times during his spiritual practice. It meant a lot to him to discover that this perspective was available at any time he chose to access it. Mimi also recalled moments in her life when she had felt free and joyful. One such time was when she and Larry had taken a hike together and found a beautiful spot by the water to sit and talk. She recalled it as a magical moment of intimacy and connection for them. While still skeptical that she could access this sense of connection when she was angry, or that it would make much difference in their relationship, she agreed to try during the next few weeks.

During that time, they each found great insight into what had been going wrong and how they could correct it. Larry saw how his frustration was making it impossible to find his loving feelings for Mimi. He realized that from out of the box he would never choose to be so angry at her, because his love was more important than his anger. Nor did his anger reflect the kind of spiritual person he considered himself to be. From this perspective, he experienced his strong commitment to the relationship. He realized how his anger and disappointment had created a deep division between them, and he no longer wanted that distance. He wanted instead to focus on creating a loving environment at home.

From out of the box, Mimi fully experienced Larry's love for her for the first time in years. She saw how his anger was really his pain. She experienced how she had kept him away from her because of her resentment about the way he was treating her and her own fear of being intimate. She accepted her part of the responsibility for the problems in the relationship. Until that time she had been denying her ambivalence about balancing career and marriage. Now she could speak about it, and Larry could hear it without feeling rejected or threatened, because he felt her love. They both experienced a renewed sense of hope and commitment.

Over the coming months, we met every two to three weeks to discuss their progress and begin to look at their vision for the future together. The pervasive anger between them all but disappeared as they interacted with each other from a respectful, caring place. Their focus turned to healing their relationship rather than creating distance and winning arguments. They often got out of the box not only to communicate in a more loving way, but also to be open to each other's needs and wants. They learned from this perspective how to listen without defensiveness or blame.

When the ego was not in charge, they were able to experience their own longing for connection and intimacy. The changes were not automatic—they were sought after and worked for—but Larry and Mimi now had the resources within themselves to accomplish what they wanted.

Larry left a message on my answering machine one evening saying that he had hoped for a miracle, and it had happened. Several weeks later Mimi called to report that their intimacy had become incredible, but she was "not going to tell me the details" over the phone.

Today they are even closer and say that their relationship has never been as loving as it now is, nor has their level of communication ever been so pure. Mimi requested and received a transfer to a position with less pressure, shorter hours, and less travel. They bought their first home and are planning to have a child.

From out of the box, issues literally melt away. They simply do not exist when the focus turns to the heart. As you can sense, all issues become workable from this perspective of caring. Couples are less willing to fight and much more willing to learn about and be open to their differences. Judgment disappears in the context of caring. Miracles happen because separation and distance disappear. Challenges become ways to deepen the relationship and deepen the understanding of each other's needs and desires.

I have often seen the way this perspective opens possibilities because the focus shifts from one of narrow self-interest to one that fosters and embraces the needs of the other. This doesn't mean that there are never disagreements—and passionate ones at that—but the context for the disagreements is one of natural and profound concern for the other as much as oneself. One's interest shifts from an often unconscious commitment to keeping everything as it has always been and seeing one's partner and oneself as unchangeable to realizing that each can change in very practical yet meaningful ways.

Remember, the out-of-the-box perspective is one that involves *taking action* rather than sitting miserably and hopelessly in pain. Solutions to difficulties are sought simply because we can clearly see their necessity. From a commitment to each other, we just don't stop until a resolution is found. This is profoundly different from being in the box, where we literally can't find our way out of a problem, so we put up with it or complain about it to our friends and powerlessly wish it would all magically disappear.

Practically speaking, the art and science of communicating from out of the box involve expanding your interest from yourself and what you can get or might lose to giving more fully of yourself. You seek new possibilities for resolution and connection and abandon old ideas that don't work. In the end you find that you get exactly what you needed or wanted all along and realize that you simply required a different way of going about getting it.

Instant exercise:

Think of a challenging issue you face with a person you care about. Ask yourself, "If I wanted to bring this relationship back into harmony right now, what would I do? What would I say? Am I willing to do things I have not wanted to do before to bring about change? Is there anything I lose by dropping my anger and resentment? Is there something I still need? If I am concerned that a similar situation might happen again with this person, what do I need to say or do to assure that it will not? Is there anything I need to ask for?"

If you still have the need to express your hurt or anger, then get out of the box and express yourself in a way that honors both of you. As we just saw with Mimi and Larry, it is a wonderful and often healing experience to express what you are feeling from your heart. You lose nothing by being this vulnerable, yet there is much to gain. Go ahead and take the risk.

During the next few weeks, make a conscious choice during challenging moments to notice the times that you would have automatically communicated from in the box. Then respond from out of the box instead. List the times that you do it. At least three times a day would be wonderful.

For example, "I was about to get angry at my husband for not taking out the garbage again. I decided from out of the box that I would not risk having a very familiar fight. Instead I asked him in a loving way if he would take it out in the next hour. I said I would really appreciate it. He agreed and actually did it. I then thanked him for doing it."

By practicing and writing about your experiences, you will really begin to build your out-of-the-box muscles. You will also learn to immediately recognize and change your unconscious and habitual responses.

Resolving Your Anger

Resolving anger and handling disagreements is the most challenging aspect of relationships. For this reason, I will expand on what I said in the last chapter by focusing specifically on resolving anger and disagreements in relationships. Remember, your ego responds much like everyone else's, so there's no reason to feel embarrassed or ashamed if you recognize ways that you may have acted in similar situations in your life. We all react in about the same way.

Anger begets anger. When you put it out into the world,

you can be sure it will come right back to you. Anger is insidious in relationships; like dripping water, it slowly accumulates and sometimes without notice and over time causes great emotional and physical damage. When you do not accept responsibility for your anger but blame others for "making" you feel that way, the stage is set for separation and pain.

How many times have you lashed out in anger, only to regret what you said? What were the costs? What if you knew that the real culprit in all this was the wounded ego—so sensitive, so judgmental, and so willing to sacrifice everything to protect itself from being hurt? In its irrationality the ego expresses itself in self-serving ways. When it doesn't get what it wants, it complains, attacks, blames, or suffers. With the least provocation, the ego gets either defensive or aggressive. Unfortunately, it is most easily provoked by those we care most about because with them it often feels more vulnerable to being hurt.

Anger may feel terrible, but at least it is familiar. Our anger keeps others away and keeps us "safely" behind a thick wall of protection. Over time this wall of protection can be hard to pierce unless we have the intention to do so and the proper tools.

From in the box, your feelings are your primary focus and concern, and for this reason they are easily triggered. You give them your power and accept them as Truth. From this perspective you *are* your feelings. There is little room in that box for the needs of another person. From out of the box, however, your focus shifts to your desire to heal your relationship or resolve a problem in the most mutually satisfying way. This guides your every response. What would previously have angered you may not even be interesting—much less important.

Roberta and Steve are a married couple in their forties going through a very difficult period in their lives. They had been trying unsuccessfully to have a baby using in vitro fertilization. They had recently undergone their third attempt and were awaiting the results. In the past, anger was a challenging issue for them because they both let it get out of hand. There was no physical abuse, but there were some close calls. Still, the problem had greatly diminished over the last few years.

They came in for a session following an angry fight that had occurred two days before. Steve acknowledged that he did not yet want to give up his anger because he felt that he was being manipulated and controlled by Roberta. Giving it up, he said, placed his well-being in her hands.

Halfway through the session, I reminded Steve that he could choose to see Roberta from his heart rather than through the intense anger that was gripping him. From this perspective (out of the box) he would be fully in charge of himself and back in control. Although he felt as if the anger was giving him strength, he began to see that the opposite was true: he was being controlled by it. Surprisingly, he was unable to sustain his anger despite wanting to.

As he saw the choice before him, he immediately softened. He began to realize that being "right" in this situation was ultimately losing. He put his anger aside, using step two of the process, and began to focus on how he would feel about Roberta if he were out of the box. From this perspective he could understand (as the letter that follows reveals) what was truly going on with himself and with Roberta. He started to feel his love for Roberta again, and this perspective gave him the control he really wanted—he was back in charge of his emotions. Now he could again choose exactly how he wanted to feel, which was to be in his heart.

Steve wrote about what had happened in the session and the things he realized later that night. His letter was poignant, and he gave it to me to include in this book in the hope that other couples might use it to resolve their difficulties.

I felt myself lying next to my wife 1,000 miles from her. Her terrible sobbing seemed to me to be only a tactic. Though I wanted to comfort her, I couldn't. To take her in my arms would be to admit that I was wrong and that I was the cause of her pain. Though I love her, though I want to be her happiness and her comfort, it seemed to me that she rendered me incapable of comforting her, by seeming to accuse me of creating her anguish. I needed to remain impervious to her manipulation. I was trapped in my growing rage, stymied by how to end the struggle without losing the fight. I had to remain vigilant. I hated her for what she was doing to me. I was trapped, unable to respond to her demands. I could not, would not allow myself to become her hostage.

In the session, I realized that her pain was not a trick. It was the depths of despair, and she was begging me to save her from it. If only she could have asked me for the comfort instead of demanding it. Two starving victims lying in bed, unable to touch, unavailable to each other, yet it was the only thing each other needed. Checkmate. Stalemate. In the box. Stuck. Suffering.

Warren suggested that I do an end-run around my resistance. Consider it an opportunity to be a hero. Listen to my heart. Respond with my heart. A shortcut. She's suffering. I can stop it. Cut through my resistance. It is my strategy for victory. "How would I respond if I were out of the box?" Can I take her in my arms? Can I roll over and say, "Roberta, I love you?" It's not a triumph over her, it's a triumph over myself, my resistance, my monsters. I come out of the cave, out of the box, where I can be useful!

The focus shifts from her pain and hysteria to my love and response. It's more useful. I love her. I want the pain to end.

The tension begins to drain from my shoulders. I begin to giggle. Roberta is giggling too. We have left the place of anger and despair and tension, by simply willing it to be so. By just making the choice to be out of the box. To say yes.

Roberta knows that if I can get through this, I'll be able to help her. I'll be strong for her, for anger is weak, and clarity is strong. She knows I can go there. She wants me to. She loves me.

This transformation is something that is incredibly powerful, stunningly simple, and deeply profound in its effect. It made me think about what is Godlike in me. I recall the St. Francis prayer that begins "Lord, make me a channel of thy peace . . . ." When I become a channel of God's wishes, I become part of God. That I can do, simply by doing it.

In light of this beautiful transformation, it is important to underscore how compelling anger is for the ego. Steve wrote that Roberta's "demands" on him made him so angry that he could not give to her despite really wanting to. The ego misinterpreted and distorted Roberta's despair as being aggression. No wonder our relationships are in the shape they are in! The resulting anger froze Steve in his tracks. Once he realized from out of the box that he could choose to focus his attention on giving to her (and being a hero) rather than on his fear and rage, he was free to express his love and also to help Roberta overcome her pain. From this choice he encountered his true heart waiting within. Then he was free.

No matter how distant our loving feelings seem to be, if we want to find them, they are always waiting just on the other side of the box. At times accessing these feelings will be quite challenging, as it was for Steve. He had to fight the temptation to stay enraged.

It's been about eight months since this session, and there have been no other such incidents. Both continue to use the process when necessary to resolve difficulties. They are now spending much of their time caring for their new infant. All are doing well.

In order not to be consumed by anger, it helps to recall the second step of the four-step process described in Chapter Three. Before you attempt to get out of the box, put the issue that is troubling you aside. When you are in the middle of an angry episode, it can be difficult to remember that there is another way to see things. It is also the last thing you want to do. You are so entrenched in the righteousness of your feelings that it is tough to let go.

Choosing to get out of the box in the face of your righteous anger or pain is an amazing, empowering, and thrilling experience. At one moment it may seem impossible to hurdle out of your emotional state, and the next moment you are on the other side.

You might not yet have forgiven the other person for what they have done (if in fact they have done anything hurtful), but you now have some distance from the feelings so that you can do what's necessary to resolve what happened. You also have the clarity to see what went wrong.

Honestly, it's still exciting to me, after more than fifteen years of using the process, to see how quickly we can shift from feeling angry to feeling fully engaged in a relationship simply by making the choice to do so. And when I look at things from out of the box, I'm still amazed that I or anyone would ever spend a moment sitting in any dreadful feeling. What's the point? Why do we to it to ourselves?

You can take control back from the emotions that have led you astray. You can do it by asking and answering questions that will enable you to look more deeply into what's going on and view the situation differently. All you have to do is use the question or questions that work best for you and have the intention to move on. The rest is easy.

Out-of-the-box-questions:

Is there a more rational response to what happened? How would I express it? Would I lose anything if I did not express my anger? Would I gain anything by expressing it differently?

What is it that I really need right now? How can I ask for it?

What do I need in order to feel that I am being heard? What do I need in order to feel understood?

Is there something that needs to change? How can I begin to bring that about?

Is there something the other person needs from me right now? Am I willing to give it?

Why do I want to stay angry at someone I care about? Why am I doing this to myself and to them? Why am I letting my ego trap me in a place I don't want to be? Who's driving this train, anyway?

What is most important to me: being right or being close?

Am I willing and courageous enough to completely drop my anger or to express it differently? Am I willing to experience the freedom that comes from doing something I've never done before? Can I tolerate the feelings of uncertainty? Am I willing to give of myself in this way? What will be the rewards?

How can I express myself in a way that reflects my true self?

Anger can also mask many other feelings such as hurt, sadness, rejection, or a sense of injustice or unfairness. Sometimes these feelings are more painful, and we would rather not face them, but the only way to resolve an issue is to understand it and face it. So it is important to look honestly beneath the surface of your feelings and acknowledge the true source of your upset. From out of the box, you have the proper perspective and enough distance to clearly perceive what is going on and resolve it. You are also interested in discovering the truth because that is what will set you free.

The following questions will help you discover what's beneath your anger. It takes some courage to do this and a willingness to resolve the upset. It also takes a commitment to get back into harmony with the person you are angry with. Use these questions to get to the bottom of your anger:

Is my anger really about something totally unrelated, like my work or my physical state?

Is my anger really masking my hurt, discouragement, frustration, fear, or doubt? Is my anger protecting me from much more painful feelings? Would it be useful for me to face these feelings from out of the box so that I can see them for what they are and resolve them?

Am I just frustrated about not getting what I want? Do I need something to change? Is there another way to ask for it?

Am I looking for an apology or an acknowledgment that I've been wronged?

Do I enjoy feeling right about being angry? Is my anger a way of getting revenge?

Overcoming Your Resentments

I had been working with Thomas and Jean for several months to resolve some marital issues. Thomas realized that he had seriously ignored Jean's needs for years. He usually liked to do things his way and had often discounted Jean's needs. From his commitment to her, he saw that he could choose to listen to Jean's requests in a way that made her feel loved by him. As he explored this new understanding, he saw that he had to repair other important relationships in his life as well.

As Thomas began to master getting out of the box, he thought of trying to use the process to deal with issues regarding his father. They had never been close. His father had always been critical and distant, and Thomas clung to his resentment, blaming his emotional difficulties on his father. One evening while dining alone with his father, Thomas realized, "My resentment served no purpose, so I made a choice to put it aside. I just did it. I decided that my relationship with him was more important than my resentment. I never realized I could do something with the feelings toward him. I can just make the emotions go along with how I want them to be."

Thomas saw that by making the choice to put his resentment aside, there was space for him to choose another way to see his father and interact with him—one that was based on resolving the old hurt and resentment rather than perpetuating it. The result was that for the first time ever, "I felt close and loving to my father." He went on to say, "I am discovering who I am. I'm not who I thought I was, but I'm still me."

Thomas realized that from out of the box, he could literally choose how he wanted to feel about his father—he could remain angry and resentful or be in his heart. This was similar to what he learned in his relationship with Jean. From this perspective, how he responded was based on his desire to be free of emotional pain and his desire for a more caring relationship. He now knows that the choice is always there waiting for him in any situation at any time.

You Don't Have to Be Nicer, Just Clearer

Being out of the box does not necessarily mean that we become "nicer" individuals or that we don't stand up for ourselves when we feel mistreated or abused. Quite the contrary. We naturally honor our needs and expect others to do the same. Nor does getting out of the box imply that we ignore our anger, or any other feeling for that matter. Rather it means that we have the clarity and the willingness to look an issue squarely in the face and see it for what it truly is.

Being nice in the face of indignity may reflect that we are more interested in being liked and in avoiding conflict than in standing up for ourselves. Acting from a sense of unworthiness and having a difficult time making requests reveal that we are accepting the ego's image of who we are rather than what our true self has revealed about who we are.

In contrast, being nice from out of the box may be a beautiful expression of our true heart. Being kind in the face of aggression may also indicate that we are committed to interacting from the out-of-the-box perspective beyond all else and that we would not surrender that commitment for any reason. This is similar to a pacifist's commitment to nonviolence, a vegetarian's commitment to not eating meat, or a parent's commitment to the well-being of their child. It is a commitment we live by each and every moment of our lives.

In my own life, I don't "unconditionally love" those who are rude or unfair to me. I usually let people know when they are treating me disrespectfully. For example, if a reservation agent or a customer service agent is rude or unhelpful, I talk to them from out of the box; that is, my intention is to change the way I am being spoken to rather than to put them down or get revenge. I simply ask them for respect from a place of respect.

Especially in the case of strangers, it is impossible to know what preceded our interaction. Was the reservation agent mistreated by another customer, or did he miss his morning coffee? In either case, I still don't deserve to be the repository for his frustration.

Freddie has been dealing with his anger and frustration for many years. He used to get really frustrated by the constant barrage of phone solicitation calls he'd get at work and at home. One evening he received a telephone call from a man who wanted to sell him life insurance. Freddie recounted that he immediately decided to get out of the box to handle this situation in a new way.

"I told him immediately that I was not interested." Not surprisingly, the salesman did not end the conversation. Freddie repeated that he had no interest in buying insurance. In the past he would have gotten extremely angry, he said, but on this occasion he did not. He told the caller, "I don't understand why you don't respect what I am saying to you." He asked the man, "What would it be like if you were home one evening and got a call, and the person disregarded what you had to say?" The caller said that he "would not appreciate it." Freddie then asked him why it was OK for him to do this to others when he himself would not like it done to him. When the salesman still persisted, Freddie said, "I really don't understand why I have to hang up on you rather than you ending the conversation as I asked."

Freddie's wife, Ilene, said that she had never heard him

be so respectful, real, and honest in such a situation. She was happy that she no longer had to worry about a telephone call ruining their evening together.

When we are in the box, we don't usually take the time to treat people the way Freddie did. Nor do we think it is possible to change lifelong patterns. We believe that these patterns are part of who we are. Look at your usual in-the-box way of responding to a difficult situation, and see how you would respond from out of the box instead.

In a similar situation with someone who is being short or impatient, you might say something like "Is there a reason why you are speaking to me like this?" Or "Have I asked a question that is really dumb?" Or "Is there something I missed?" Or "Are you really having a tough day?" People will usually apologize for what they said and immediately change their attitude, and the anger is diffused.

When I do this, I am being respectful while at the same time maintaining a standard about how I deserve to be treated. I want people to see for themselves how they look and sound to me. I assume they also feel grateful that they are not getting the same treatment they are dishing out. Most people are relieved to drop their frustration and anger for a moment. Our true selves do not want to be angry. So I just speak to people's true self rather than their ego. I am never disappointed. Both of us are left in a better place as we experience the possibility of being free of upset that exists in every moment. See if this is true for you.

I am suggesting that you can always respond from out of the box, no matter what another person is doing. Responses from this perspective are always more clear, powerful, and certain than when you join the other in the box. Nothing is gained from that.

Resolving Deeper Hurts

Mike is a very successful architect, respected around the world for his innovative designs. As a child he was sexually and physically abused by his father while his mother stood by. The stories were horrendous, and there were many repercussions in his life. He was extremely afraid of intimacy, and he was prone to rage with the least provocation. He has been married for ten years to Barbara, an attractive, articulate, loving college professor of English literature. They have no children.

When Mike and Barbara got married, she was aware of his family history but felt that they could create a nurturing marriage together in which he could finally feel safe. She supported him through long periods when he needed to withdraw from her emotionally. But when his anger turned to rage (he threw a toaster across the room during an argument), she decided she could no longer be part of a world that was so full of pain and unhappiness. She never stopped loving him and was always able to imagine him free of his childhood shackles, but she felt that they needed to get help or to separate. That's why they came to see me.

Before they could reestablish any level of intimacy, Barbara needed to feel safe again. They had not had sex for almost three years, and the level of tension between them was extremely high. Barbara was frightened that Mike could again become violent. Mike was angry because he felt so rejected.

Given their emotional distance and anger, I wanted them to get outside the grip of those emotions to view the situation with clarity. Given how hopeless and angry they both felt, it was too soon to focus specifically on what had happened during the last incident.

I thought that it would be useful for them first to do something within themselves and then together. I taught them to get out of the box. It was especially important for them to put their anger aside in order to experience this state of mind. This was more difficult because they had each come to the session so deeply immersed in their anger and resentment. In spite of this, they were courageously willing to try something that I felt could help them relate to each other with less tension.

After they each experienced being out of the box and feeling free, I asked them if there were any moments in their life when they had sensed a similar feeling. Barbara recalled a time when she experienced a wonderful feeling of being safe and warm on a beautiful beach in Maui. She also remembered a spiritual experience she'd had. Mike recounted a moment earlier in his life when he felt a spontaneous connection with God. The recollection of it put him instantly back in that experience.

As Mike began to get in touch with his heart, a beautiful transformation came over his face. It was so moving and so profound to see this shift that I've always wished I had videotaped it. From a commitment to staying in this perspective, Mike felt a deep connection to Barbara and to his love for her. He apologized for his abusive treatment of her and promised never to do such a thing again. Barbara accepted his apology but appropriately said that she would leave him if he ever threatened her again. She also said that this was the man she always knew he could be. It was not a magic end to all their problems, but it was a deep and profoundly moving beginning.

In the coming months, Mike experienced many instances of getting out of the box and had a long list of questions he would ask himself to facilitate it. For instance, he would ask himself, "If I felt my love for Barbara right now, how would I respond?" Or "If I felt my love of God, what would I experience?" Or "What if I knew I were worthwhile just as I am? How would I see things? What would I do?"

During one session, he mentioned that he felt his anger was sometimes justified (although it was much less intense than it had been in the past). We decided that in that situation he would get clear by asking himself, "What would God think about my anger right now? Would God think it was justified?" Mike found that these questions gave him the perspective he needed to shift to his heart.

The three of us continued to meet together to resolve a number of issues. Both Mike and Barbara often used the process to resolve difficulties that came up. Mike wanted to continue to examine issues concerning his childhood in individual sessions, which we did. From his deepening understanding of the out-of-the-box perspective, he could clearly see the hurt that his childhood had caused him throughout his life. He also found that at the most challenging times, when he was most apt to retreat into old patterns of fear or anger, he could instead make the choice to respond from his heart and not from his pain.

From in the box, letting go of the past may sound like glossing things over, denying your feelings, avoiding your hurt, thinking positively, or being callous to your real pain. None of these is the case. From out of the box, you see the reality of what has happened to you. You are not putting a positive spin on it. It was what it was. But you can make the choice to respond to it from your desire to be free of it.

We all encounter people in our lives who are hurtful, disrespectful, or mean-spirited. It may be a lover, boss, family member, or friend. From in the box, we might blame ourselves for triggering anger or disrespect, carry resentment to our grave, or believe that we have been forever damaged by the event.

There are other reasons why we might not have let it go: We might feel justified in our anger. We might want to teach the person who hurt us a lesson. We might not be able to stop ourselves from replaying the scenario in our head (assuming that we want to), or we might have been unaware that we had a choice. You might want to use what you learn in this section to begin to reexamine your reasons for holding on. It is important.

Hurt and anger linger because we continue to focus on what happened in the past and see ourselves as well as life from that vantage point. We repeatedly tell ourselves what is wrong with us and listen very closely. We identify with the pain. We forget that much has changed since we first assessed life when we were younger.

The ego likes to view life from the past. In the past there is certainty, albeit with a great deal of hurt. Why not begin to update your files and dump what is no longer useful? Why not begin to see what happened as something that need not affect your present or future? What if you saw it as already past, done, gone? How would that be?

When we do this we are not denying our true feelings, because our true feelings are those that show up when we are out of the box. From this perspective we understand the choices we have—to suffer or to be free.

From the clarity of this perspective, we know that whatever has happened to us could never permanently erase our awareness of the truth. It just got clouded over. No matter what has happened, our true self remains pure and untouched. The ego is what gets hurt, not us. Look deeply into this matter to see for yourself if this is true.

Some of you have been through very traumatic events in your childhood and later life. You may have been abandoned, raped, the victim of incest, adultery, or sexual and/or emotional abuse. Your parents may have been alcoholics, drug addicts, or mentally ill. The list could go on.

My purpose here is not to discuss the issue of whether to forgive what has happened to you. You must decide this for yourself from out of the box. If you *choose* to look at what happened from out of the box, you can begin to live your life in a very different way.

Using this process, you will realize that you can find a place in yourself that is undamaged and unscarred by whatever happened to you. From this perspective, I invite you to look at what occurred and decide how you wish to interpret it from here on. Is it really true that you are damaged? If not, what role if any will the events of your past play in your life? I trust what you discover from this perspective. I trust that you will as well.

You will probably realize exactly how traumas, if they were not resolved, influenced your beliefs about yourself and your life. But when you look from this new clarity, you will see exactly what you now need to move on. You'll also be equipped to do so. You will know, at the deepest level of your soul, that you are unscarred. The work will be to live from this knowledge when the going gets tough—when your emotions are triggered by challenging situations. The question will be, "Will I respond from who I am or from my old image of myself?" With practice and your intention to change, you will learn to make the right choice. Many others who have experienced the worst of childhood traumas have already learned to do so.

Out-of-the-box questions:

If I were not my wounded ego, who would I be? How would I define myself? What would change in my life?

What if I were truly unscarred? What would that say about my responsibility for my life, my responsibility for being happy, my responsibility for being successful, my responsibility for being free?

If I were out of the box, would I want to work this out with the person who hurt me, or would it be best to do it myself?

If you want to work it out with them—What do I need to say to or hear from this person to move on? And when will this encounter take place?

If you can work it out yourself—What if I saw myself as whole and complete? What would that say about my being scarred? Would I be willing to leave this old image of myself behind? Who then would I be?

If you choose to work this out within yourself, look directly at the injustice that was done to you and realize from out of the box that it could not have any effect on how you see yourself or on the life you want to live. Many have gone beyond their abuse, and you can too.

Become absolutely clear from out of the box why this is so and how you will do it. Just don't stop! Good luck.

Deepening Intimacy and Sexuality

Your ego is fully invested in keeping you comfortably safe and distant from others. In that separation it is secure and protected because, like armor, separation wards off any threat of hurt or disappointment. Because of this you often settle for too little, especially in your most treasured relationships. Perhaps you have not realized that so much more exists. Perhaps you are afraid. You simply have not realized what is possible and therefore accept an intimacy that emanates from your ego and from your sense of separation. This denies the possibility of true intimacy except at those wondrous moments in your life when you feel at one with another.

I invite you to explore much deeper levels of oneness in your lovemaking. Here is the way I would describe those moments: You know there is no difference between you as you merge into one. You trust this powerful force of love as it envelops you. It takes you for a ride that feels like floating in the sky with the clouds. You are weightless and safe and full of love. You surrender to a place of trust. All you are is the deepest expression of love—nothing more, nothing less. Once you enter this place, you know it is real and that it is the most wonderful gift you could share with another. Wherever you are in your intimacy at each moment is the perfect place to be. You need nothing more.

At these special moments when your ego vanishes and your true self is expressed, you see that your perception of reality has always been terribly mistaken. There is really no separation between us. You can know this very deeply and with absolute faith. How different life would be if only you could consistently tap into that place.

True intimacy exists not only between lovers but also between friends and even between family members at those rare moments of vulnerability when your defenses come down and you choose to be together without pretense or fear. It can be sought when you are willing to deeply trust the other as yourself, when you know there is nothing to hide and nothing fundamentally wrong with who you are. Then you can risk coming out into the light of day and being yourself. It is quite rare indeed, but I and many others have experienced it, so I know it's possible for you.

Achieving this state of awareness is a deeper level of being out of the box, and it is truly worth everything you've got. I know I am perhaps asking more from you than I should this early in the process. I could simply have suggested that you get out of the box and be more loving, which would be great. Instead, I want to offer a new possibility that you may not have known exists.

I want to challenge you to discover new possibilities for yourself. I hope you get out on the skinny branches and respond with a sense of abandon. It is only then that you might achieve the states of oneness, intimacy, and sexuality that are possible.

Here are some questions to help you understand this place:

What if I chose to trust myself and another as never before? What would that mean? How would that feel? How would I be?

If I felt no self-consciousness and no limitations, what would I express?

If my body took me where it wanted to go, where would that be?

If I surrendered to the energy of love, where would it take me? Would I let go?

If we were one, how would that be expressed?

If I were free, could I bear to be out of control? Could I trust the great mystery of life that much? Will I do it?

If I were fully in my heart, how would my body express itself?

How can my body express my love?

What if I knew I were completely safe? How would I respond?

How can I give completely? How can I fully receive? What if there were no separation between us? What would that reveal?

What if I trusted that at the moment of sexual intimacy, I was exactly where I needed to be and so was my partner? How would that be?

What if I trusted that even without words, we were feeling the exact same sense of oneness?

A Vision for the Future

Each time you choose to get out of the box in order to find the truth about what you feel, what you did, or what another has done to you, you are really choosing to triumph over the human condition. This is evidence that you want to know and fully understand what is occurring instead of simply reaffirming what you already know or thinking that you are right. You are being open to life and its mysteries. It is a wonderful and exciting way to be. This is a far cry from our customary way of being together and may reflect the next phase of human development on this planet. Each of us has an important role to play in this evolution.

The questions I ask you to consider throughout the book always emanate from this vision of where we're going. It might be helpful to trust that there is a force of nature that is also helping you along the way. This force of evolution seems to beckon us back to our true self. By calling upon your own true self, you will discover much greater fulfillment and the true source of peace. You might also find that your relationships begin to express a genuine concern and caring that you may have thought was reserved for the saints among us (of which there are all too few).

7

Stop Eating Your Heart Out

The Epidemic of Food Issues

> Making the connection is understanding that it is not food, it is about the way you live your life—all of your life—and your willingness to change the way you live your life. That's what the connection is.
>
> —OPRAH WINFREY, MAKING THE CONNECTION

Relationships with others are indeed complex, especially from in the box. But for many people their relationship with food is no less complicated and consumes as much attention. For some it is the most challenging issue in their life.

Hannah is a very bright thirty-four-year-old single woman who works with emotionally challenged adolescents in the New York City schools. She is extremely committed, feisty, and well respected by both students and administration. She goes after what she wants and usually gets it. Hannah is a bit less successful in her relationships with men and with food. She is very attractive but would like to lose about seventy pounds. She has taught me a great deal about the many issues involved with food.

During one period when she lost more than fifty pounds, Hannah was extremely uncomfortable with the attention she was getting from men. She didn't like it at all and wanted to put the weight back on to create a distance between herself and the unwanted attention.

There were also times when she would eat an entire pie or a large bag of potato chips at a sitting. This would always be when she was upset about something that had happened at school or with a man she was dating. Eating replaced dealing with the problem.

Hannah learned to call upon her "higher self," whom she called Maya, when she sought the wisdom she needed. Maya always knew what was best for Hannah and was an incredibly loving, accepting, supportive resource for her. Although Maya was always there waiting, Hannah had to be willing to accept her love and ask for it at challenging times, even though it may have been the last thing she wanted to do. Maya, of course, was Hannah's fully out-of-the-box self, always there, always waiting, always right.

Hannah continues to stay focused on her health each day. She knows it is something she will always have to do. She has learned to face what upsets her rather than burying herself in food. She also knows there is much more to learn about herself. But she is determined to win what seemed like an impossible struggle—taking charge of her weight and her mind. I have complete faith in her.

Hannah represents a significant portion of the American population who are also struggling with being *fat* (the politically correct term for being overweight). People are obsessed about their weight, while the numbers of those who are fat is steadily increasing. There are many issues affecting how and why people eat, and we will address some of them in this chapter.

"Americans have developed bizarre behaviors around weight,

eating, and food in the late twentieth-century. . . . Many people feel and express guilt rather than pleasure, when they eat." This statement comes from an excellent book called *Worth Your Weight*, written by a respected colleague, Dr. Barbara Altman Bruno. She serves as the Mental Health Advisor for NAAFA (the National Association to Advance Fat Acceptance). She goes on to say:

> Americans' fear of fat—in food or in one's body—results in a wide range of strange and sometimes disturbing behaviors:
> - In Los Angeles, where appearance is everything, anyone who wants to be taken seriously eats only vegetables, fruits, and grains—sans fat—in public.
> - Some fat children are killing themselves rather than endure socially-accepted ostracism in school.
> - Dissatisfied with how they compare to media images of exceptionally thin, young models, and fearing looking older or "too fat," thousands of adults and adolescents have sought plastic and gastric surgery.

Hating your body, obsessing about food, or judging yourself and others because of weight is a sign of in-the-box thinking. It has nothing to do with reality. For example, recent research indicates that there is a weight or body-fat "set point" for most people that the body vigorously defends, despite how much you eat, starve yourself, or diet. If you are having trouble getting your weight below this set point, it is *not* a psychological matter and there is *no* emotional deficit that you're trying to fill.

You might consider a certain weight to be excessive, and unfortunately the current standards in society might even agree, but physiologically your weight may be exactly right for you. The reality is that size 14, not 8, is the average dress size for America's women, even though you would never know it from the fashion magazines. Feeling badly about yourself for not conforming to some implanted image of how you "should" be is a symptom of in-the-box thinking.

The psychological aspect enters the fat equation when you experience depression, apathy, loss of sex drive, or starving and bingeing in connection with your body image. If you think you have a weight problem, the first thing you should do is *not* to begin starving yourself. It is to closely examine your relationship to food, and its meaning to you. And the best vantage point for this exploration is one that is very far away from the box.

Instant exercise:

To begin this exploration, it would be helpful to uncover your in-the-box reasons for eating. Here are some. Add your own.

1. To nurture yourself
2. To numb yourself to emotional pain
3. To protect or distance yourself from others
4. To avoid feeling the pain or loss of a relationship
5. To avoid feelings of unworthiness
6. Because you never learned to "listen to your body" (which knows which foods and how much you really need)
7. Because you got into the habit
8.

9.

10.

You probably have a variety of reasons that you use at different times to absolve and justify your eating—many people do. The point is to face your specific reasons for eating inappropriately so that you can make more rational choices. There is much at stake in regard to your emotional, physical, and spiritual well-being.

Eating In or Out of the Box Tonight?

The fundamental question to ask yourself is "Are you in or out of the box in regard to how, what, where, when, and why you eat?" If you discover that you are in the box, then it is important to recognize the many tricks the ego will use to keep you from using this process. Here are a few statements you can count on:

> *This will never work.*
> *I'm destined to remain fat.*
> *I can't do it.*
> *I hate this out-of-the-box stuff!*
> *It won't last.*
> *It's too hard.*
> *I've tried everything.*
> *Why try?*
> *There's no hope.*
> *Where's the next chapter already?*

From in the box, you always tell yourself to start tomorrow—a surefire way to maintain the status quo. For example, when I was growing up, my mother used to say each week that she would start her diet on Monday. She was only slightly overweight, but she still let her ego rule her. As I remember it, the only thing that began on Mondays was school.

Eating Your Way Out of the Box

Here are more familiar excuses you may have heard *other people* use regarding food to justify their irrational eating habits. (You may possibly have said similar things to yourself.) Use the examples to help you examine the ways you have rationalized your own behavior. As always, add your favorites as you recall them.

In-the-Box Statements	Out-of-the-Box Responses
I will definitely start eating better tomorrow.	Doesn't today seem like a perfectly fine day to begin?
It doesn't really matter.	What if it really did matter? What would I do then?
I deserve to eat this food.	How does my body deserve to be treated?
I've had a tough day today. Why not eat what I want?	How can I treat myself and my body really well right now?
Chocolate would make me feel better.	What else can I do to treat myself well?
Just this once.	Wouldn't it be a great time to begin an entirely new way of responding to my needs?
I don't care.	What if I cared deeply? What would I put in my mouth?
They say everything makes you sick or causes cancer anyway!	What if I really got serious about my health? How would I eat?

Now write your own in-the-box rationalizations and your out-of-the-box responses to them.

Keeping It Up, and Getting It Down

When you decide to resolve your weight and eating issues, the age-old questions remain, "How do you sustain your intention to act from what is best for you rather than from what your ego wants, which after all is comfort, immediate satisfaction, pleasure, and relief from the pain of wanting? How do you stay focused and committed?"

From out of the box, you know what is right and best for you, and you naturally have the fortitude and self-interest necessary to carry it through. This will be true on those days when you want to do what you set out to do and also on the days when you don't. One reason is that even if you occasionally falter, your commitment to your well-being will take precedence over the droning complaints of the ego.

You will also be in a state of mind in which you are already satisfied and fulfilled so that the emotional relief that comes from gorging yourself with unhealthy foods will be unnecessary. This does not mean that you will eat only rice, beans, and vegetables (unless you believe this to be right for you). It means that your decisions will be based on a clear certainty of what's good for you.

Instant exercise:

From my commitment to myself, what would I eat for lunch and dinner today? How much would I eat? When would I eat? Where would I eat? Will I commit to doing precisely what I know is right today?

Remembering to call upon this clarity will be challenging. For this reason, I often suggest that clients adopt the habit of getting out of the box before deciding what to eat at each meal. For many it is helpful to plan their food the night before (or even earlier for some) so that they do not get stuck in the dilemma of being "starving" and unwilling to take the time to make appropriate food choices.

Instant exercise:

Consider the way you usually eat and ask yourself, "If I were out of the box right now, what would be fueling my desire to eat? Is my body hungry? If it's not hunger, what is it? What can I do for myself that would resolve the issue more appropriately? How else can I nurture myself? Does what I put in my mouth truly nurture my body? If I were truly listening to my body, what would it be saying about the food I should be eating?"

By asking these questions you will know whether you are eating because you are hungry or to comfort yourself because you are not feeling so great, or if something else is driving the behavior. From out of the box, you naturally eat a good healthy diet that nurtures you emotionally and physically.

You will no longer be run by the needs of your ego, which may want to keep control by making you feel powerless.

Final Thoughts

1: Keep your sense of humor about all of this. That will be especially helpful if you tend to be really tough on yourself about your weight.

2: Acknowledge yourself for being honest and willing to see yourself anew. Acknowledge how hard you've worked at this before. Recall what worked for you in the past, and incorporate that into your plan. Then go for it with an intense commitment to being triumphant, no matter what! Just don't stop.

3: You don't have a unique or special problem. It is the human condition. Do you know what segment of the population overeats? You can trust that most people have some sort of in-the-box behavior regarding food. There is nothing to blame yourself about and no valid reason for doing so. You now know better.

4: Ask for whatever support you need, whether or not you feel ashamed or embarrassed to do so. Working together with another person is an excellent idea.

5: Call upon the wisdom of your true self by getting out of the box. It will tell you the right thing to do. It always has your best interests at heart—literally.

8

The Box and Your Health

Illness is a reminder of the purpose of life.
—GOTHARD BOOTH, IN *YOU CAN FIGHT FOR YOUR LIFE*
(LAWRENCE LeSHAN)

Because the crisis of illness is so shocking, it can force us to reexamine long-held beliefs or habits. At these times it no longer makes much sense to wait or deny what may be wrong in our lives. Nor does it make sense to accept our previous excuses. From the new perspective that illness brings, life appears quite different. I can't tell you how many clients have said that without their diagnosis of cancer they would never have made the profound changes in their lives that they were so grateful to have made.

From out of the box, it is hard to understand why it takes a life-threatening disease to make healthy changes in our lives. That's the irrationality of the ego. Does it really have to take a bolt of lightning to wake us up? There must be a better way.

Our health is intimately connected to the expression of our life. When we live with a sense of constriction, negativity, fear, and doubt, our body is more likely to crumble under their weight. When we live with a sense of satisfaction, happiness, fulfillment, and love, we are doing our part to promote our health.

There is no longer any excuse to live as if we didn't know the effects of our attitudes and emotions on our body. The evidence is everywhere. Wonderful books, such as *Healing Words* by Larry Dossey, *The Immune Power Personality* by Henry Dreher, *Cancer as a Turning Point* by Lawrence LeShan, *Love, Medicine and Miracles* by Bernie Siegel, *The Healing Journey* by O. Carl Simonton and Reid Henson, and *Spontaneous Healing* by Andrew Weil, as well as many others, are excellent introductions to this fascinating topic. The information is supported by thousands of studies showing the link between mind and body. They reveal what we all know intuitively, that the mind plays a role not only in ulcers, headaches, heart attacks, and back pain but also in less understood illnesses like cancer.

Stories of remarkable recoveries from serious illness, much like the ones I will describe in this chapter, are abundant. They exist. We must begin to open our minds to a new acceptance of the role of the mind in healing if we are finally to make great strides in medicine.

I have divided this chapter into two sections. The first focuses on what you can do to *regain* your health and how to use out-of-the-box thinking if you are confronting a serious illness. I will describe the triumphant story of a woman named Beth who was diagnosed with cancer in 1991. Her prognosis was uncertain. I began working with her right after her diagnosis, and we continued to meet for the next few years. Beth wrote diaries during that period, and I've included writing from them as examples in case you wish to use diaries for your own healing.

The second section will be dedicated to *staying* healthy. I will give you several tips and suggestions, drawing upon what I have learned over the past twenty years from many inspirational people with whom I have worked, who used their illnesses to heal their lives. There will be much that you can apply, whether you are working to stay well or working to heal.

Section One

Getting Healthy

We can go to the best physician, eat the healthiest organic foods, exercise till we drop, and drive the safest car, but if we are not taking care of our inner life, we are putting our health at risk. Our body becomes the repository for our unresolved issues. So we need to clean up our act from within.

For example, if instead of dealing with challenging issues in our personal relationships, our family, our work, or in ourselves, we simply shoved them into different pockets of our coat, after a while the weight of these burdens carried around day after day would make them difficult to bear. It never occurs to most people to try to lighten the load until the body cries for relief. This is the way the body works. The heavier the emotional and physical load, the greater the likelihood that the body will succumb to illness. The structure that holds it all up, which is our body, will eventually give way under the stress.

The Protective Mechanism of Being Out of the Box

Let's look at stress from in and out of the box. From in the box, the stressful effects of life come right at us unobstructed. When we are in the box, it is as if everything that permeates the walls also permeates our skin. We delude ourselves if we think that we can escape these harmful emotional effects.

From out of the box, it is as if the ill effects of our environment cannot breach the protective barrier that surrounds us. We respond to life from a powerful commitment to being free and from that commitment are impervious to the harmful effects of stress. Our true self will not respond to stress in ways that overwhelm or hurt us. It will simply do what needs to be done to maintain our equilibrium. We stop being a victim of the effects of life.

It is as if, like a radio, we are tuned to a different station and cannot receive the signals of life's stresses. Our life may still be essentially the same, but we respond to it in a very different way. We are no longer receptive to anything that takes us away from our true heart.

From the clarity we gain by returning to who we are, we realize a commitment to our well-being that will not allow us to stray into the land of pain and suffering. We quickly realize the harmful effects this mistake would have on our emotional and physical well-being, and that understanding guides us to the most appropriate attitudes and actions.

Our commitment to this new perspective also encompasses an unshakable commitment to living a healthy life. Our true self naturally champions that cause and acts relentlessly to defend against any challenge by a frightened ego. The only responsibility we have is to set our true self free, to allow it to do what it was created for—give us a life that reflects the miracle of our birth.

When we confuse ourselves with our ego, stress gets trapped inside and weighs us down. When we cease to operate from our ego, the "stressful" effects of life paradoxically become mechanisms of emotional healing. See for yourself with the following exercise.

Instant exercise:

Ask yourself, "If I were out of the box, how would I view a stressful issue in my life? What would appear different? How would it affect me? Will I choose this new perspective?"

From out of the box, you will transform the way you view your stresses. They will either become sources of satisfaction or you will drop them. You will access a strength and certainty that is unshakable. You will be solidly residing in the truth and will be able to resist fearful, worry-filled thoughts that are irrationally based. They will not get onto your radar screen, which is tuned to receive only life-promoting signals. The energy-draining effects of fear and worry will be eliminated from your body. They will be replaced with the recognition that you are competent, strong, and fully able to handle the challenges of your life.

So from out of the box, stress dissipates and freedom and wisdom arise. Wisdom allows you to make distinctions between what is useful to attend to and what should be avoided. When you avoid the harmful effects of powerless and victimizing thoughts, you are free to shift your attention to health-promoting attitudes toward life. These include the realization that you can choose a more meaningful and satisfying life and satisfy your longing to be free.

Overcoming Your In-the-Box Beliefs about Health and Illness

There is still a great deal we do not understand about the body's ability to heal, but it is pretty clear that more is involved than taking pills, having surgery, and rigidly maintaining your lifestyle. Healing clearly involves your attitude and the way you are living your life. If you do not address these matters, it's like tying one hand behind your back while trying to climb a ladder. You may make it OK, but why take the risk? Why not summon all of your resources to make it to the top?

One of the most beneficial ways to release your natural healing resources is by resolving what is not working in your life. One crucial area to examine is your in-the-box beliefs about your responsibility for getting sick and getting well. It's time to examine them so that you can eliminate the useless beliefs and replace them with empowering ones. Even if you're not currently facing an illness, see if any of the following beliefs and replies ring a bell.

In-the-Box Health Beliefs	Out-of-the-Box Responses
I can't do anything to change my health.	What can I do right now to start healing? What will give my life meaning? What do I want to live for?
I'll never get well.	How can I possibly know this? No matter what illness or disease I have, there have definitely been others who have gotten well from it. What will I do to be one of them?
Why did this happen to me? What did I do to deserve it?	I may never know why this happened to me or if I "deserved" it. What I do know is that there is much I can do to get well. That's what I will focus on. That's what will make the difference.
Nothing of value can come from such a terrible thing.	What lessons has the illness already taught me about myself and my life? How has it affected the way I'm living? In what new ways am I already appreciating life?
It's really my fault that I got sick.	Given that I will never know if this is true, what is the most useful way to mobilize my immune system? How can I strengthen my resolve to be well? What will I do?

In-the-Box Health Beliefs	Out-of-the-Box Responses
God is punishing me because I [fill in the blank].	Because I can't be certain what God is thinking, how can I best live in a way that expresses God's spirit from now on? How do I imagine God wants me to live? How does God want me to treat myself?

How do you decide what areas are unhealthy for you? One simple yet clear way is to ask yourself either of the following sets of questions:

Instant exercise:

If I were my body, what would I need in order to stay healthy? Would I prefer to live from in or out of the box? For what reasons? How would it affect my health? How would I want others to treat me? How would I treat myself? How do anger, fear, and hopelessness affect my health? How stressful is it to deal with these things? Are there circumstances in my life that are equally burdensome for me?

If I were diagnosed with cancer today, what areas of my life would I change? How would I change them? Would it matter if the changes were difficult? Would I still undertake them? Must I wait for an illness to do what I know is healthy for me?

The Triumph of Beth

In 1991 a thirty-nine-year-old woman came to see me after being diagnosed with mesenchymal chondrosarcoma, a soft tissue cancer of the cartilage. Our first session was one month after her surgery to remove a tumor the size of an apple from beneath her shoulder blade along with two-thirds of two ribs where cancer was also found. During the surgery, radiation seeds were implanted at the tumor site. Beth was about to begin a five-week course of additional radiation treatment.

At the time of her diagnosis, Beth had been married to her childhood sweetheart for seventeen years. They had a seven-year-old boy named Andrew and a two-year-old girl named Isabel. Beth was doing an internship for her graduate degree as a school psychologist. She had worked as an art teacher with special-needs children for the past ten years. Like most working parents, Beth dedicated herself to juggling the needs of her children, her husband, and herself.

After she learned she had cancer, her worst childhood fears arose. When Beth was five, her mother had suddenly died of a stroke, leaving her father with three young children to raise alone. She had always feared that her children would be left in the same way.

When I told Beth I was writing this book, she offered to give me the diary she kept during the time we worked together. She hopes that the lessons she learned and the profound changes she made will help others to meet their own challenges. It is important to remember that this is the way *Beth* approached her illness and used the process. Each person uses the process in their own way.

Beth did not need to change her marriage, her career, or her relationship with her children. She did need to resolve her approach to life, which was predicated on a kind of negativity and hopelessness about ever being truly happy. It involved the sense she had that she, like her mother, would inevitably have her life cut short by a serious illness. This all changed as she worked hard to recover from the cancer and began to appreciate life anew.

Beth's diary reveals the way the out-of-the-box process helped transform her life. Her writing is emotional and reveals how she felt about herself, her cancer, and her life. Initially, Beth focused on her fears:

Anxiety is getting worse—constant worry, distraction, obsessed about right side, and too petrified to do anything about it. Can't even do affirmations because my head is screaming, "Already recurred!"

In the first session we focused on identifying Beth's in-the-box thoughts and feelings:

The box is dark, ugly, craziness, based on old habits and childishness. It's not what is real.

After our first session, her diaries began to change:

Don't deny feelings. That's when the body will react, therefore I must acknowledge all feelings. When I feel crummy, worried, scared, or fearful, I will shift to out of the box. . . . Take a stand. Fight back. Make a commitment to my life. Focus on right now! Is there anything to suffer about in this moment? NO!!

Interrupt crazy thoughts—look to see the truth, rather than seeing what I'm seeing—it's out-of-the-box faith in self.

As she got further into our work together, she had an easier time controlling her anxiety:

When stuck in the box: Take deep breaths and ask "If I were clear, how would this look? How else could I perceive this, respond to it? Is this what is happening now, or am I making myself crazy with scary stories?"

The out-of-the-box me is the strong one who will pull the sniveling, crouching, whining, and frightened me out and into the sunshine. The out-of-the-box me is very very very strong!

When I'm clear I see my panics, etc. as so much laziness, indulgence, self-stimulation, and misery. When I'm clear I hear what people say to me, I can focus completely on what is outside me. I see the world. I enjoy it. I slow down my pace. All is quiet on the inside. I can turn my attention out. It's a great place to be.

When I'm out of the box, my fears seem very silly, stupid, childish, and pointless. A real indulgence—I'm on the wagon now—no more of this, and it's beyond being for my health— now it's for being happy, living my life, enjoying everything to the fullest. If I am out of the box I can take the time to be quiet, and clear my thoughts. It's not hard. I stand taller, sit straighter, have more enthusiasm and energy. I think about things differently.

Everything is delicious and to be savored and enjoyed. Whatever the weather, the light, the color of the sky, each activity is a treat.

Once Beth was able to experience life from out of the box, she was open to the lessons one can learn from the crisis of a serious illness:

I am learning to be different, to live differently. To be positive, to embrace life—my life. To be an optimist, to be assertive, to be clear, to have clarity, and to be happy. To make my head so healthy my body must follow. To learn lessons from my body.

My body got sick because I was too filled with loss and pain and hurt, and envy, and misery, and jealousy, and I was able to have that miserable collection of misery get hard [the tumor] and cleanly removed [by surgery]. Now that I was lucky enough to get rid of it, I must make sure it never returns.

Scary thoughts, twinges, and fears are OK if they are gotten rid of in five seconds. Be confident and buoyant that you are and will continue TO BE WELL!

Beth's final entry was written five years after her diagnosis:

How fitting to be at the end of this journal, for it really is the close of a chapter for me. . . . I've learned to define myself, to assert myself, to handle fear and panic, to be joyful, to be myself, to stand up for my life, notwithstanding tremendous support from friends and family. A lot of terrible stuff happened to me and I have withstood and even thrived! I have found broken pieces of myself that were too painful to bear and reinserted them. I am so blessed and so happy and so lucky and so strong. What a process this has been. Thank you G-d for enabling me to get here today. Amen.

It's important to remember, especially at times when you have a serious illness, that the natural response of the body is to heal. Like Beth, your job may be to remove all obstacles in your life that obstruct the natural healing process. This means facing your life honestly and fully and doing all that is necessary to be well emotionally, physically, and spiritually. This is exactly what Beth was able to do.

The Healing Path Revealed

Not only does the out-of-the-box perspective reveal who you are, it also reveals the way to your healing. You begin to realize the many ways you have not been true to yourself and how you have either settled for less than you want or given up having more. From in the box you accept so little.

That's what the ego wants you to do—to hope for a better day but do little to achieve it. There is nothing else to do from inside the box except to hope and dread!

When you are out of the box, you begin to experience a deeper connection with life and with others. You begin to see how little time you have and how important each day and each moment are. You stop waiting for life to grab you, and you begin to live it with a powerful intensity.

From out of the box, a new world of possibility opens up. You are no longer *stuck* with anything in your life. This includes your history and your emotional upsets. You see everything as contributing to what you need to learn to get well. Everything becomes grist for the mill. That is your one-pointed intention.

It's an important but tricky point. If you are truly out of the box, committed to your healing, then whatever you do will support your healing as well. Your actions will reflect your singular intention.

If you really want something, then no "obstacle" will stop you. Like a mother who raises a car off her child, you may discover powers you were unaware of to accomplish a miraculous feat. If your intention is clear, then what you do will forward this intention. The seeming obstacle of an illness will be the perfect way to discover aspects of yourself that had remained hidden throughout your life.

From this clarity you also begin to *know* what the body needs to get well and what you need to do to carry it out. This knowing and determination to heal override the fear of changing and wanting to keep things as they are. They begin to compel you to change in ways you know are right and healing for your body and your soul. It is all you want.

When you listen, you begin to respond to a higher calling—a

calling that has your highest interests in mind. This calling cares little for your excuses and reasons for why you can't have what you yearn for. You are able to see the excuses as merely the voice of the ego. You stop listening to the hard-driving, endless demands and begin to look from a more rational, compassionate perspective. You then set out in the right direction without regard to your cynical and fear-filled doubts.

Being Trapped and Getting Sick

Many people who become ill report that in some significant way they feel a sense of being trapped or stifled in an important aspect of their life. They may or may not be aware of it, but it is revealed as they discuss their life. It may be in a variety of areas, including their work or relationships, or within themselves.

It could, of course, be said that many of us feel a sense of being trapped in some aspect of our lives, but the feelings seem to be much more pronounced in people who get sick. In *Cancer as a Turning Point*, Larry LeShan has called it a "thwarted creative fire." He believes that it primarily reflects difficulties in one's work or in one's artistic expression.

In a conversation he and I had, I said that I thought the experience of being trapped also extended to other aspects of one's life. He didn't disagree but said that his focus on one's work might have to do with his "puritan ethic." In either case, I think it is extremely important, whether you are healthy or ill, to look into all aspects of your life where you feel a sense of being stuck or discouraged. Here's some help.

Instant exercise:

Find an area in your life in which you feel discouraged or trapped. How do you see it from in the box? Is there much room to move? Do you have many options? Now ask yourself, "How does it appear from out of the box?" From this perspective what options do you have? What can you do differently to change what is going on? What effect would it have on your body? What will you do to end this suffering?

Alternatively, you might ask yourself, "Are there any areas in my life in which I am not fully expressing who I am and not realizing my hopes and dreams?" It might be in your work, your relationships, your spirituality, or within yourself. If so, ask yourself, "What can I do to bring about a profound change in this area over the next year or two? How might this affect my emotional and physical health? What will I begin to do? When will I start?"

Norman Cousins, in his book *Anatomy of an Illness*, pointed out almost two decades ago that there are literally hundreds of hormones that are released from the brain in response to emotions. What you feel affects your body. It is probably also true that certain feelings and beliefs are more likely to play havoc with your immune system than others. For example, your body can easily deal with short periods of hurt, anger, stress, and discouragement. In fact, in small amounts there is probably nothing harmful about any of these feelings. It would certainly be better for most people to experience and then resolve the causes of these feelings rather than to deny or ignore them.

The problem is that when these feelings are not dealt with, they begin to pervade your very being. They become the lens through which you perceive and respond to life. They are always with you. Your body never gets a break. You can imagine how this might drain your body's energy and vitality. It is your responsibility to see that this does not happen, or if it has, to change your perspective right away. Your ego is all too happy to remain in a broken-down state. It is pretty comfortable there. It knows exactly what will and will not happen. Everything is firmly in hand.

The following entry from Beth's diary illustrates this point:

Why do I think suffering is good? Was I taught that suffering yielded some reward? I nail myself to a cross. Why do I do this? Do I not deserve a healthy life? I do not need to suffer to pay for being happy, and if I do this I am being nuts!

Are there ways that you live with similar paralyzing thoughts and fears about yourself or your future? If so, work to resolve them as soon as you can. Examine them from out of the box to see if they're anything more than ghost stories you tell yourself.

From in the box, you see no way out. You believe that the fear or hurt will remain a part of your life forever. The discouragement is palpable. Once you get out of the box, you can see before you the path to changing your attitude about your life circumstances and/or the circumstances themselves. You stop procrastinating and suffering over what is wrong. There are options, and you grab them.

Prescription for Health

If getting scared and sick woke me up, then good! Wake up, enjoy your life and your health.
—BETH'S DIARY

Cancer just stops everything for us; we can drop all the worries and the pressures of life, and some of us get that it's an awakening to what life can really be. I think that makes the difference.
—FELICE, A CANCER SURVIVOR

From a clear perspective, be willing to examine all aspects of your life, as difficult as that may be. From here you will discover what needs to change. This includes aspects of your relationships, work, diet, exercise, and your attitudes about your life and yourself. Why not develop a plan to change your behaviors and beliefs so that your body is not forced to inform you, in its own inimitable way, what must occur? (Remember, illness is not a necessary requirement for change.) When you are clear, you know what is right.

I would like to end this section with some of the questions I typically ask clients to think and write about. They are designed to uncover what your primary focus of healing should be. I invite you to use them in the same way for yourself. Be as specific as you can.

Healing questions:

If I were fully committed to my health right now, what would I do? How would I treat myself? What aspects of my life would I want to change? What obstacles or excuses for not changing seem to melt away? How would I begin? Would I have any reason to blame myself for anything?

If my illness were truly a gift, what lessons would I be learning from it about my life, my body, and myself?

If I were being deeply compassionate with myself, how would I approach my illness? How would I see my future? What would help me to get well: my trust in God, my belief in my own healing capacities, my sense of connection to something greater, my trust in my physician, or something different? Could I let myself imagine getting well?

What would my body need from me? How will I satisfy it?

What role would love play in my healing? How will I increase it?

How will every aspect of my life be an expression of healing? How will I manifest it?

In the second section of this chapter, you can build on what has just been discussed to support your body in staying well. By living the most satisfying and fulfilling life you can, you will be doing your part to maintain and even fortify your health.

Section Two

Staying Healthy

Imagine trying to make crucial life decisions if your focus is split among your fears of making a mistake, your insecurities, your self-judgments, your history of failures, your doubts, your worries, and your indecision about what is truly best for you. This is the way most people are on a good day. These concerns are playing in the background much of the time while you make important decisions regarding your health, career, relationships, and future. It is easy to understand how you make poor decisions, even when you think you know the right way.

Instant exercise:

Imagine that there was no compelling background noise and that you were clearly able to see the choices before you in an important area of your life. What would you do? What if you knew that there was one right way to go and you were able to discern it? What would it be? What if your ego was not shouting at you and, even if it were, you were totally uninterested in what it had to say? How would this affect your making the right choice for your emotional and physical health? What if your choices were based on what supported your well-being and a deep concern for the well-being of others? How would you live your life? What would you do? How do you think your level of stress might change?

From out of the box, this is the way things are because you are able to make decisions with great wisdom. You can see things as they are, without the ego's distortion. Life can be good.

I strongly suggest that you commit to a plan for transforming your health. This means examining all aspects of your life—including your diet, work, relationships, exercise program, and ways of relaxing and enjoying yourself—from a clear place. All of these things can and will affect your health. You can begin with the question "If I were out of the box and committed to my health, how would I change my life?"

From this perspective, you can easily decide what to do. Take it one week at a time, and focus on those areas you know are unhealthy. If doing this alone or getting started seems overwhelming, then do it with someone else, or tell someone what you are doing so that they can monitor your progress and remind you of your commitments if you "forget." This person should be someone you trust completely to have your best interests at heart and someone to whom you can confide your usual ways of avoiding what is good for you. Remember, taking small steps can be as important as taking larger ones. Do it by yourself. Do it with a friend. Just do it. Action is all that matters.

It is important to distinguish between health-opposing and health-promoting behaviors as you ask and answer questions that will change your life. In fact, now's a great time to ask yourself, "Am I doing anything in my life that isn't health-promoting?" If the answer is yes, ask yourself, "What changes do I need to make right now to turn that around?"

From out of the box, you will know that it is appropriate to honor your body by eating well. With this in mind, you will replace poor eating habits with a healthy diet. Similarly, you will recognize that it's time to get off the couch and begin an exercise program (with your physician's approval). This is the eve of the twenty-first century—we all know the value of exercise. Only your ego denies this knowledge and offers reasons not to. You will also stop complaining about a boring life or a mundane job or how difficult it is to change, and you will actively pursue what is most rewarding and enjoyable in every area of your life. These would be natural out-of-the-box responses, right?

Creating a Health Journal

I suggest that each morning you create the kind of day you want to have by asking and answering questions to shift your perspective. In the evening you can review how successfully you used the process to resolve issues and create a more satisfying day.

If you do at least three or four things each day to promote a sense of well-being, it means that in 365 days you will have done between 1,095 and 1,460 things (give or take). You'll be so healthy! It's like putting $5 in a bank each day. At the end of the year you will have $1,825 (not to mention interest). After ten years, you can imagine how profitable putting all those good things into effect would be for your body.

Each morning choose one or more of the following questions to focus on throughout the day. The questions are designed to change your behavior in ways that will support your health.

From out of the box, what three things will I do today that will be health-promoting emotionally, physically, and spiritually?

What will I do to shift my negative, frustrated, resentful, hopeless, or powerless attitude and behavior today? (For example, how will I stop being angry at my lover, hopeless about money, frustrated about my career, or powerless about my health?) What will I do to change these things?

What old way of being will I drop today? (For example, will I interact with [fill in the blank] from a place of compassion rather than anger or judgment?)

What contribution will I make today to another? Will I listen without being judgmental? Will I be more loving? Will I give from my heart?

How can I have more fun today? How will I lighten up?

What healthy food will I eat today?

What will I do to get beyond my sense of being overwhelmed at home or at work?

How will I express my passion today? In what areas of my life?

How will I stop suffering, worrying, and complaining today? What will I speak about and do differently?

What will I contemplate, read, or do that will further my spirituality today?

What else will I do today that I know will be emotionally healthy for me?

If I knew that my health was truly in my hands, what would I do to ensure it?

What can I do to make today the healthiest day of my life? If it's not possible today, when will I do it in the next two weeks?

In the evening, think about the day you just had and ask yourself, "What did I do today that promoted my well-being?"

List the new out-of-the-box responses you made and actions you took during the day. It would be good if you could recall at least three.

The Extraordinary Lessons from Cancer Survivors

> Illness may be seen as a step on life's way that brings us
> in contact with who we really are.
> —DAVID ALDRIDGE, "IS THERE EVIDENCE FOR
> SPIRITUAL HEALING?" (*ADVANCES*, 1993)

Before I wrote the first words of this book, I knew that I wanted to include this section. It doesn't quite fit the form of the other sections, but the message of these survivors is one that I feel blessed to be able to share: Life is a precious gift. Live each day accordingly.

Cancer survivors, on their own, discovered the meaning and purpose of life. They found what it meant to be happy, satisfied, and whole—their health demanded it of them. They reached down deep inside and sometimes even beyond. What they found was that the answer to life is—yes.

In presenting what they said, I could have formulated it as in-the-box and out-of-the-box statements, but I felt it was important to let them speak directly to you and for themselves. What's more, you now understand the place from which their statements arise. So sit back and enjoy the miracle that calls forth their words, knowing that this place resides in you as well. The place is revealed in a life lived out of the box.

Whether you are facing an illness or not, there is much you can learn from those who have looked into the face of death. Remember, these are "ordinary" people who made extraordinary changes in their lives. Much more than a temporary shift in awareness, the understanding that arose revealed a way of living that went far beyond one's usual sense of limitation and fear. It expressed being free.

As you read their words, you may want to keep the following questions in mind:

How does what they are saying reflect out-of-the-box thinking?

What do these stories teach me about living my life from this perspective? In what ways am I willing to change?

In my study, completed in 1994, I interviewed thirty-three people (eleven men and twenty-two women) from around the country who had been given very bleak cancer diagnoses but who had greatly outlived their prognoses or totally eliminated the disease from their bodies. They ranged in age from twenty-eight to seventy-eight. All were given less than a 20 percent chance of recovery by physicians. Most were considered to have a 5 to 10 percent chance of recovery. I wanted to know what *they* thought contributed to their survival. The results were surprising in many ways (and are discussed in greater detail in an article published in the journal *Advances* [Berland, 1995]).

Although thousands of studies have pointed to the role of psychological factors in illness and healing, only three or four had ever asked survivors themselves what *they* believed contributed to their healing. I thought that the patients could best understand and explain what factors played a salient role in their recovery.

For many, cancer offered a new perspective from which to view their life. They often said that it changed their life for the better. As Bruce put it, "I found that cancer was a real growth experience. The truth is I'm glad I had it. God forbid I ever have to do it again, but it was an incredible teacher—an incredible teacher."

What happened to the people in this study? Typically, they began to take more time for themselves. They began to look for a much deeper satisfaction in their work, their relationships, and in life itself. They began to surround themselves with people who promoted a sense of well-being and let go of aspects of their lives that did not. They came to intuitively understand what fostered their healing, and they did it. They found new careers and hobbies. There was nothing that could stop them.

Richard is a married, very successful businessman, who was given two years to live in 1974. Over the years, he has written vast numbers of letters in response to those seeking his advice on how to get well. He said that anticipating helping others gave him meaning and purpose in his struggle to recover.

There were times when I was pretty near gone. I'll say this, I believe one of the most profound things that hit me was that the experience was so difficult that I thought I just don't believe the universe works this way. There's got to be some good that comes out of this. If I can just stick it out and get through this, then I can help a lot of other people. So I began to think beyond myself. It was very powerful because I would then say, "OK, now when I get well, I'm going to do thus and so." Instead of focusing on "I'm sick, I feel bad, the doctor said, I'm going to die, your blood counts are down, blah, blah, blah," instead of thinking like that, I started thinking, "How best could I help other cancer patients?" . . . So as we speak today, I've sent out well over 100,000 letters.

Richard's out-of-the-box response not only helped him to cope with the illness, it also helped many others.

I've had the good fortune to get to know some of these truly remarkable people. Their lives were made even more remarkable by the way they met the adversity of a life-threatening illness. I hope that by hearing what they say, you will be inspired to make the out-of-the-box health and life choices that you *know* will promote your well-being. Maybe these changes will also play a role in keeping you well.

Three Approaches to Healing

After a careful review of the interviews, it became clear that there was no "right way" to heal. Instead, a pattern emerged in which participants fell into one of three categories of response to their illness. One group relied primarily on attitudinal and/or behavioral modifications (changing their attitudes and beliefs to become more life affirming). A second group was predominantly composed of "determined fighters" (this group felt they'd literally waged a war against their illness). A third experienced a shift in their spiritual or existential orientation, which they believed played a role in their recovery.

Many in the first group said that they would be willing to examine ideas and beliefs they'd previously rejected out of hand. Roz, a fifty-eight-year-old university professor diagnosed in 1974 and expected to live for two to five years, said:

> [I am] becoming more open to ideas that I don't understand. . . . I am becoming more empowered in situations where I would normally have given up. I don't accept any authority now, very little—and so it has changed me, has made me stronger and powerful. There's no question about it. . . . I am less trying to please others or to follow others. . . . I think that having the cancer made me realize, hey, you're not going to live forever. If you find something—a relationship that's good, that's what counts.

Many others in this group discovered a new appreciation for life and a willingness to enjoy it. Surviving this ordeal revealed the preciousness of life's many blessings. Many everyday occurrences took on special meaning and pleasure, as they did for Elaine:

> I think it's changed me because I look at things so realistically now. I mean, you could tell me the worst story in the world and I'll say, yep, OK, and I don't cringe from facts like certain people do. I tend to look at every day as what it is, and not be deceived by it. I'm happy that I can see another day. . . . But it has turned me around to the fact that I am happy being around people I like and my family and my friends, and I won't deny myself the privilege of being around them.
>
> I enjoy each day for what it is, whether it is raining or not. People complain of rain. Well, yeah, so the flowers grow. I'll stand out in the rain sometimes. I love the rain to drip on my head. Some people think I'm weird. . . . But I have been happier because of my illness, I have been happier—in my way of enjoying life. I enjoy stupid little things or big things. I get a kick out of things more than I would have if I didn't have this particular sentence behind me.

Almost half of those in the study said that they were more likely to express their needs as a result of this experience. They believed that learning to request what they wanted and express what they felt was a healthier way to live. Mimi, a happily married social worker diagnosed in 1971, exemplifies this change:

> I would say, for the first time in my life (not for the first time I could remember, for the first time in my life), I could consider that I had some legitimate needs and they were OK to be met

first. . . . I could make my own choices, I could change doctors, I could find my own doctor—I guess it was kind of like a sense of win or lose, I was living in a different way—that whether I died or not was not as important as the fact that I was finding other ways to live, which were much more satisfying.

The ten participants in this first group said that they took an active role in their recovery and changed their attitudes about themselves. From this perspective, they did whatever they felt was necessary to support their healing. They took charge of their lives, even in ways that had been challenging before.

Of the eleven men in the study, five comprised the second group. This group said that they focused their attention and attributed their recovery to "fighting to survive." For these men, their fighting spirit seemed ingrained. Most of their discussion involved metaphors with allusions to the "battle" or to "fighting." I therefore called them "determined fighters." They spoke unhesitatingly of the importance of maintaining their current lifestyles, and never getting caught up in fear or worry. They did not attribute their recovery to any psychological or spiritual changes in their lives, nor did they undertake therapeutic help. In fact, I believe a few of them would rather have died than see a "spiritual teacher" or therapist.

For each of the five men in this group, healing was not attributed to a shift in their view of themselves or their approach to life. It came about by their determination to get well. Jerry, a former truck driver, was the only person in the study who attributed recovery *entirely* to "medical treatment." His interview lasted about fifteen minutes (most lasted about one and a half hours). These words capture his approach: "What are you going to do, man? Sit in a corner and cry? I feel fortunate that I can still function. I haven't given up nothing or changed anything." He recommended that others "force themselves to keep themselves up . . . get your mind on other things." His demeanor indicated that the likelihood of his ever choosing to be in a "support group" would be about nil. The approach taken by this group was in stark contrast to the men in the last group, who attributed their recovery to profound spiritual changes in themselves.

More than half the participants in the study (eighteen) attributed their healing, in large measure, to a spiritual shift in their perspective on life. These participants believed that changes on a level that was deeper than attitudinal were necessary to recover fully, and they oriented their lives toward bringing about such changes.

For some, the changes altered their sense of meaning and purpose. For others, a profound shift occurred that transformed their understanding of who they were and brought about the realization of another dimension of reality. Their perceptions about their lives clearly took on a new texture, and all of them reported a sense of feeling fulfilled and of being a part of something larger than themselves.

They claimed to have been forever and deeply changed by the transformations that occurred. Most became psychologically stronger, intent on following their own strivings and unwilling to compromise their beliefs. They felt that their lives and well-being depended on remaining true to their new understandings about themselves and their priorities. They began to live a life committed to the expression of what they considered their true nature. All claimed that when they did this, life became more satisfying than they had ever known was possible. This is exactly what you experience when you are out of the box.

Doris, the spiritual psychotherapist I quoted in the introduction, who was given one year to live twenty-three years ago, said:

When you can connect with that center within you that is never touched by anything, the experience of life can be transformed. . . . If only you can stay in that.

She called it "that center within you that is never touched by anything." I think we all know by now what that place is, and its power to shake our world to its core, not to mention its power to heal.

She went on to describe her "total transformation" this way:

Before cancer and after cancer, the body's the same, and some of the shadows in me are the same. But the rest is gone. It's really like a total transformation. Total. I'm sure the seed must have been there. But there's no words to compare. . . . It was a process. I did not really decide I was going to do it. I think the difference was when you change your attitude, you change a lot of things because you see things differently. So it's not so much that you make a decision to change your career or to change your marriage status. It is that in the process of evolution as you change, you change the size of what fits you.

From that perspective, Doris did not need to "make a decision to change." It was a natural expression of what she had seen and who she had become.

For many of these people, their illness appeared to prompt their transformations and their ongoing commitment to new priorities and a connection to something greater than themselves. Many reported the experience of being unable to turn back to their older ways of coping and living. Their lives now appeared to have a one-pointed focus—to live in accordance with their true natures, to reset their priorities to reflect this awareness, and to maintain this commitment to themselves at all cost. They believe their lives depended on this. This is the essence of being out of the box.

We cannot say with certainty whether such radical changes were important or even necessary contributors to physical healing among these participants. It will be up to future researchers to decide that question. We can say with certainty that those who have been through this have strong beliefs and ideas about what helped them heal. Hopefully, their words will make a difference in your life and the lives of many others. These people had no greater hope than that.

Clients with whom I have worked, and many of those whom I met through this research, beautifully described the essence of the out-of-the-box perspective. It is revealed in a life filled with passion and a freedom that can arise only when you are outside the shackles of the ego. The people I have described have discovered meaning, purpose, and joy in their everyday life and were willing to change in accordance with this discovery. When it came to their health, nothing less would do. The crisis clearly facilitated this new understanding of who they were and how life could be lived. It teaches us all that it is possible at any time, whether we are healthy or not, to choose to live from this knowledge.

The question you might now ask yourself is, "How can I live *my* life with the same sense of passion, purpose, and possibility? What kind of life would that be?" That's about as out-of-the-box as it gets.

Epilogue

The fire in your heart must burn brightly. That fire will give you all the energy, strength and presence of mind to bear with, understand and ultimately see through your own mind. That fire will be your meditation and in that fire your ignorance, which is all your wrong ideas, will burn.

—ANDREW COHEN, *ENLIGHTENMENT IS A SECRET*

We end this book where we began, in deep gratitude and awe at the possibility of living our lives in a most extraordinary and satisfying way.

Of all the processes you have learned in this book, beginning to recognize that you are not your ego is the single most important first step. The necessity of this is reflected in the writings of Ken Wilber, the prolific writer about Eastern and Western spiritual thought. In the highly regarded magazine *What Is Enlightenment?* Wilber writes that it is imperative to take steps along the way in order to achieve a total transformation. These steps should be taken "in preparation for, and as an expression of, the ultimate transformation into the always-already present state."

The intent of this book has been to open the door to this transformation by examining the two most fundamental spiritual questions: "Who am I?" and "How shall I live?" For those who are willing to go all the way, such an inquiry is essential. In discussing the possibility of going all the way, spiritual teacher Andrew Cohen said in a public teaching in New York City:

In terms of what is possible for you spiritually in this life, it's entirely up to you. If we believe, "Well, I'm not ready yet," then that's going to be the case.

But the same person can say, "Wait a minute. What if I were ready?" Then in that moment all things become possible. Because when you begin to contemplate the possibility of actually being ready right now, everything opens up. Literally! I mean this in all honesty.

Where we're at is just a psychological position in relationship to our experience. That is all it is. "I'm ready. I'm not ready. I'm free. I'm not free." It's all a psychological position we take with thought, in our own minds, in relationship to our experience. That's what determines where we are. That's all it is. It's nothing more than that. It never has been, never could be anything more than that. . . . So the question I always ask people is, "How free do you want to be?"

In order to achieve this freedom, we must accept that the thoughts and feelings that we identify as ourselves, and which we hold so dear, are not us. The feelings of fear, worry, insecurity and happiness, for example, reflect a mechanistic response to life (the ego's), rather than an expression of our true self. When we embrace this realization, our feelings lose their hold on us. Our responsibility, despite the threat to our ego's security, is to make room in ourselves for the force of this understanding to come through. It is that simple, and that challenging. We then choose to respond to life from what we know to be true: that we are free, we have always been free, and that we are a part of something larger.

What if this were true? What if no matter what you were feeling at any particular moment, this perspective was absolutely yours for the asking? What if your true self were already there in all its magnificence? What if you realized that all that was blocking you from this realization was the thinnest veil of doubt? What if you refused to accept this doubt any longer? What if you were living life out of the box? What actions would you take? What would your true heart say?

When you simply ask and answer the right questions, and don't waiver an inch until your perspective begins to shift, you are lead to a place of clarity, compassion and freedom. Then you can naturally live a life of great meaning and purpose. This is my greatest hope for you. This is my hope for all humankind.

> When you discover the True Heart you will know how to walk through life with courage and dignity. When you discover the True Heart you will know what you are doing here.
> —ANDREW COHEN, *ENLIGHTENMENT IS A SECRET*

Index

Index